DRAWING TYPE

AN INTRODUCTION
TO ILLUSTRATING
LETTERFORMS

Alex Fowkes

Rockport Publishers
100 Cummings Center, Suite 406L
Beverly, MA 01915

rockpub.com • rockpaperink.com

First published in the United States of America by
Rockport Publishers, a member of
Quayside Publishing Group
100 Cummings Center
Suite 406-L
Beverly, Massachusetts 01915-6101
Telephone: (978) 282-9590
Fax: (978) 283-2742
www.rockpub.com

Library of Congress Cataloging-in-Publication
Data available

ISBN: 978-1-59253-898-0

Digital edition published in 2014
eISBN: 978-1-62788-050-3

10 9 8 7 6 5 4 3 2 1

Cover Art: Alex Fowkes
Design: Paul Burgess at Burge Agency
Artwork: Pete Usher

Printed in China

ACKNOWLEDGMENTS

I would like to say a huge thank-you to all
the contributors who have been so kind as
to send me their work, answer my questions,
reply to my emails, and generally be attentive
and patient throughout the process; this
book would be nothing without you all
bringing it to life.

Also, I want to thank my editor, Emily Potts,
for giving me this opportunity, being very
patient, and helping me throughout the
process. To everyone else involved at
Rockport Publishers, the high quality of
this book is a credit to you.

Finally, thanks to everyone I have worked
with—from tutors at university, to fellow
collective members, and employers. In my
relatively short time in this industry, so
far, you have all helped to inspire and
motivate me.

ABOUT THE AUTHOR

Alex Fowkes is a designer based in London,
who graduated from Nottingham Trent
University in 2010 with a degree in graphic
design. Alex became freelance in 2012
with his first job for Sony Music, creating
a 1,614-square-foot (150-square-meter)
typographic mural for the company's London
headquarters. Since then, he has worked for
a range of international clients, creating
a print campaign for Fila in Japan and also
working closely with pop star Olly Murs to
create a residential mural in his home.

CONTENTS

SECTION 1:
INSPIRATION & INTERVIEWS

SECTION 2:
DRAWING TYPE

INTRODUCTION

This book was created out of a love for playful typography. I would define *playful typography* as combining lettering and illustration, forgetting the rules associated with traditional typography, and letting the message and creativity take over. Throughout the book, we look at four different styles of typographic work, from hand rendered to vintage, playful to contemporary. All of these varied styles of typography can communicate on many different levels, making it quite a unique medium in which to experiment. Illustrative typography mixes illustration and typography to create pieces of work that have many layers. These compositions can range from beautiful hand-drawn pieces to digitally designed work for a range of print and online media.

Lettering is a growing trend, whether it's hand drawn, digitally created, or a combination of both. This work is now popping up in editorial pieces, packaging, product design, advertising, and motion graphics. The first section of this book features some of the world's best lettering and type designers. They talk about their inspirations and how they create their type designs—whether by hand or on the computer. Many show the steps they take when concepting and sketching out rough ideas, revealing a sneak peak at their creative processes. There is a variety of styles and techniques that will inspire and inform your work.

The second section of the book is a workshop on type basics. Using existing typefaces as a starting point, you can begin to create a whole range of type-based work incorporating different styles. I see this workshop as a personal exploration; tracing existing typefaces is just the first part of the exercise. In the end, I want you to have gained enough confidence to never touch the specimen sheets again. After all, type created from specimen sheets is not original or unique. These should be used only for personal development, not in actual projects for publication or commercial purposes.

There are sixteen type sheets that include samples of four sans serif, four serif, four script, and four display faces, in both uppercase and lowercase, that you can tear out and work with. By using tracing or layout paper, you can draw the letterforms and begin to understand how they are built and how they work. This will also help you become familiar with different type categories and how they work. Once you have completed this multiple times with each typeface, you should be able to start drawing your own letterforms and layouts freely. These exercises will help you develop your own unique style, which can then become part of your body of work.

ALEX FOWKES
MAMMOTH TYPE INSTALLATION

BELOW:
SONY MUSIC TIMELINE
DETAIL: EACH LETTER
FROM EACH WORD IS
ITS OWN UNIQUE DECAL.
ALMOST 1,000 NAMES
ARE ON THE WALL AT THE
HEADQUARTERS.

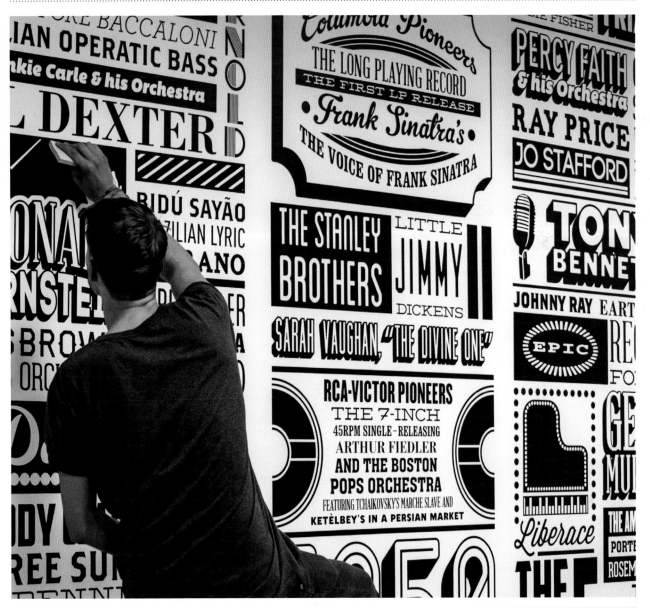

In 2012, I was commissioned to create a typographic installation at Sony Music's London headquarters.

The installation is a timeline that features the names of nearly 1,000 artists signed to Sony Music and its affiliated labels, from the foundation of Columbia Records in 1887 to the present day, including musical icons Elvis Presley, Jimi Hendrix, Bob Dylan, Bruce Springsteen, Janis Joplin, the Clash, Michael Jackson, and many more.

Interspersed among the artist names are certain key developments in recording technology, musical formats, and corporate history—from the invention of early recording cylinders, the Sony Walkman, CD, MTV, and the introduction of digital streaming services.

The work is organized by decade into 52 columns measuring more than 6½ feet (2 m) tall and covering almost 493 feet (150 m) of wall space. It uses CNC-cut vinyl as the sole medium for the whole installation. It took about two months to design. I created all 52 columns in Illustrator. I never really planned much in terms of the look of each column;

I let that come as I created it. I often work this way—setting rules and adhering to them throughout the process—so it's consistent, but it also allows the design to be natural and evolve. The placement and distance of the columns was all planned out quite meticulously, however.

LEFT:
PIN-UP BOWLING ALLEY
POSTER: THIS WAS THE FIRST
PROJECT I COMPLETED WHILE
WORKING FOR TIMBA SMITS.
THE PIN-UP BOWLING ALLEY
IS A POP-UP BOWLING ALLEY
WITH A '50S FEEL. MY TASK WAS
TO CREATE A TYPOGRAPHIC
POSTER THAT WOULD PROMOTE
THE DATE AND TIME OF THE
FIRST EVENT.

BELOW:
FILA TENNIS ADVERT:
FILA (JAPAN) APPROACHED
ME TO CREATE A SERIES OF
SIX TYPOGRAPHIC PIECES FOR
ITS SPRING-SUMMER SEASON.
THE TWO THEMES WERE GOLF
AND TENNIS. I WANTED IT TO
BE QUITE A LIGHT AND BRIGHT
COLOR PALETTE.

LEFT:
FIXED & TWO:
I COLLABORATED WITH
NORMAN HAYES OF WASTE
STUDIO ON THIS PROJECT.
THE ILLUSTRATION WAS
FEATURED IN FIXED
& WHAT'S SECOND
NEWSPAPER AS THE
CENTER SPREAD. MY PART
OF THIS ILLUSTRATION
WAS CREATING THE
SLOGAN AND MAKING
SOME FUN ILLUSTRATIVE
TYPOGRAPHY TO
WORK TOGETHER
WITH THE CHARACTER
ILLUSTRATIONS.

SECTION 1
INSPIRATION & INTERVIEWS

CHAPTER 1

HAND RENDERED

MANY DESIGNERS MAKE TYPE THAT IS HAND RENDERED TO A HIGH LEVEL OF FINISH. TYPE DESIGNERS USE A RANGE OF TOOLS, INCLUDING PENS AND PENCILS, MARKERS, BRUSHES, ERASERS, RULERS, AND PAPER. COMPUTERS MAY BE USED IN THE LATER

MATTHEW TAPIA
HONOLULU
WWW.MATTHEWTAPIA.COM

MATTHEW TAPIA IS A SELF-TAUGHT GRAPHIC ARTIST BORN AND RAISED IN HAWAII. OVER THE PAST DECADE, HE HAS HONED HIS SPECIALTY IN HAND LETTERING, WORKING IN NEW YORK AND HONOLULU FOR A DIVERSE GROUP OF CLIENTS. NO MATTER THE PROJECT, EACH STARTS THE SAME—WITH PENCIL AND PAPER.

RIGHT:
DO YOU SUFFER
FROM INSOMNIA

I tend to look at historical references as a basis for most of my work, and I had the opportunity to do just that on this project. I was one of a group of artists invited to create a piece honoring different aspects of an icon's life and career. I was drawn to Michael Jordan's much-documented love of fine cigars, and having always enjoyed the look and feel of vintage cigar boxes, I wanted to be true to that aesthetic while still bringing a slight twist to the work. After multiple rounds of sketches to develop the composition, I ended up inking three versions of the final artwork. These were scanned into Photoshop, and the best bits of each were put together for a final mock-up, then printed and transferred to a koa wood board. The finished look was achieved by hand burning each line of the artwork into the wood using a technique called pyrography.

RIGHT:
ZOO YORK GRAPHIC

BELOW LEFT:
MICHAEL JORDAN
ILLUSTRATION

BELOW RIGHT:
LONELY PEOPLE

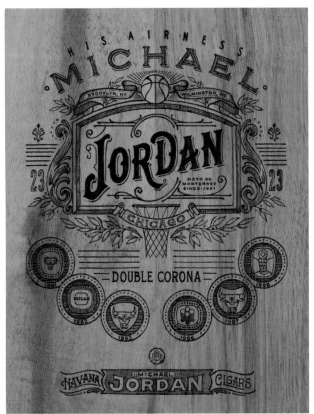

OPERA78, FIODOR SUMKIN

PARIS

WWW.CARGOCOLLECTIVE.COM/OPERA78

FOR MORE THAN FOURTEEN YEARS, FIODOR SUMKIN HAS WORKED FOR PUBLISHING HOUSES, PRINT MEDIA, AND ADVERTISING. HIS LIST OF CLIENTS INCLUDES NIKE, PROCTER & GAMBLE, ABSOLUT, WWF, AND AMNESTY INTERNATIONAL, TO NAME A FEW. SUMKIN LOVES TO FLIP BACK AND FORTH BETWEEN THE WORLDS OF COMMERCE AND ART, AND IN SO DOING, DERIVES INSPIRATION FOR NEW CREATIVE IDEAS. HE IS KNOWN FOR HIS FREEHAND GEL PEN DRAWINGS. THIS SPECIAL SCRIPT IS DISTINCTIVE FOR ITS TANTALIZING GRAPHIC MIX OF HAND-DRAWN LETTERS AND FIGURATIVE MOTIFS.

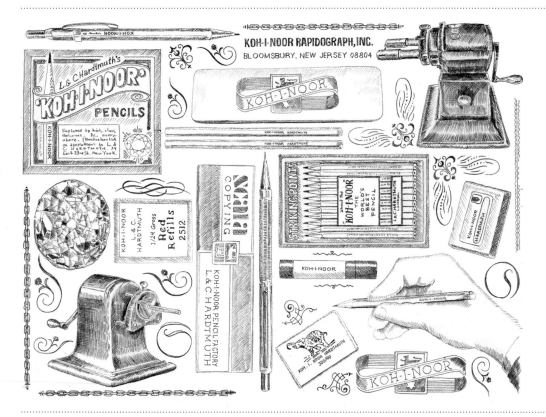

LEFT:
KOH-I-NOOR, *ESQUIRE* MAGAZINE

RIGHT:
THE FRENCH TOUCH

PANCO SASSANO
MAR DEL PLATA, ARGENTINA
WWW.PANCOART.COM.AR

PANCO SASSANO IS A GRAPHIC DESIGNER AND ILLUSTRATOR WHO IS PASSIONATE FOR TYPOGRAPHY. HE IS A PARTNER AT SMART! GRUPO CREATIVO, WHICH SPECIALIZES IN IMAGE DESIGN AND VISUAL IDENTITY. WITH THE DESIRE TO CONTINUE LEARNING, HE EXPERIMENTS IN HIS LEISURE TIME WITH MURAL PAINTING AND LETTERING TO EXPAND HIS VISUAL SKILLS AND KNOWLEDGE.

I love chalk because it allows me to work freely and easily erase mistakes. Even though there is a lot of improvisation, I always do a first draft where I make the general decisions—mainly on elements' distribution and design. Then, I work on the chalkboard with guidelines and grids that are useful to respect proportions and to take the draft to its final size. Once the design matches what I had in mind, I start working on the details until I get to the final result.

RIGHT:
CHALK LETTERING
FOR CONGRESS

COMING SOON, JIM VAN RAEMDONCK

WETTEREN, BELGIUM

WWW.COMING-SOON.BE

BELOW:
VIB FIFTEEN YEARS

AFTER STUDYING GRAPHIC DESIGN AT THE ARTEVELDE INSTITUTE IN EGON, JIM VAN RAEMDONCK WORKED AS A GRAPHIC DESIGNER AT SEVERAL SMALL AGENCIES BEFORE FOUNDING COMING SOON IN 2003. TODAY, THE BELGIUM-BASED STUDIO EMPLOYS A TEAM OF FOUR, ALONG WITH SEVERAL INTERNS FROM ALL OVER THE WORLD. THEIR WORK IS VERY TACTILE.

Modus is the membership magazine for the Royal Institution of Chartered Surveyors and is the UK's highest-circulation, property-related B2B title, mailed ten times a year to more than 95,000 chartered surveyors. There are also quarterly editions for Asia and the Americas. *Modus* focuses on the bigger picture and employs a bold mix of photography, illustration, and typography. We were commissioned to make the cover in chalk for the March "learning" issue.

We decided to make this really big, working on it with a team of nine people. After this project, we started www.theblackboard.be because we received a lot of requests for chalkboard lettering.

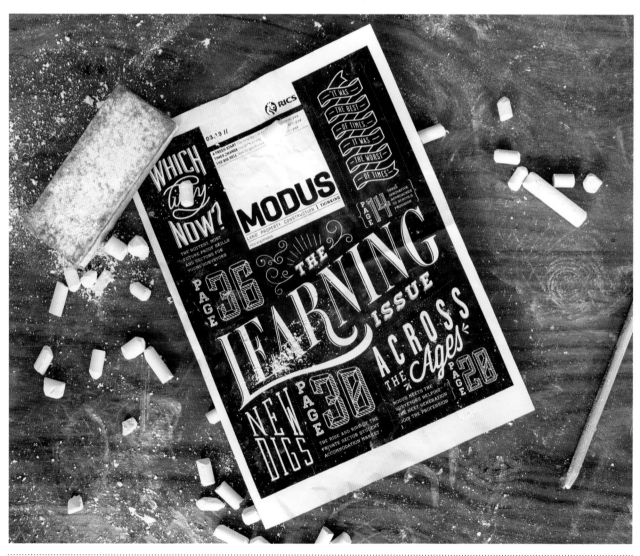

SÉRGIO BERGOCCE

SÃO PAULO, BRAZIL

WWW.SERGIOBERGOCCE.COM

SÉRGIO BERGOCCE IS A GRAPHIC DESIGNER, ILLUSTRATOR, AND LETTERER, AND ONCE WORKED AS AN ART DIRECTOR AT *MACMAIS* MAGAZINE FOR FOUR YEARS. CURRENTLY, HE IS A FREELANCE DESIGNER, WITH A FOCUS ON LETTERING AND TYPE DESIGN.

For these spreads in *Women's Health* magazine, I drew the letters over the photographs. After all sketch adjustments, they were scanned and finished on the computer. In order to keep the original aspect of analog process, such as gestures and imperfections, the letters were not retouched or vectorized.

LEFT:
FASHION TRANSITION
WOMEN'S HEALTH
MAGAZINE

LEANDRO SENNA

NEW YORK CITY

WWW.LEANDROSENNA.COM

LEANDRO SENNA IS A BRAZILIAN DESIGNER FROM SÃO PAULO, LIVING AND WORKING AS A GRAPHIC DESIGNER IN NEW YORK. HIS CREATIVE PROCESS ALWAYS BEGINS IN HIS SKETCHBOOK, AWAY FROM COMPUTERS, RULERS, OR GRIDS.

LEFT:
LEANDRO SENNA
VARIOUS LOGOS

I developed this quick project during the 2012 Summer Intensive Course at Parsons. I love observing people on the streets—there are many interesting characters out there, each with his or her own story. The most challenging aspect was asking people if I could take their picture. Once I had a good range of images, I selected the ones I liked best and wrote my interpretations of their inner thoughts with a pencil over tracing paper. Then, I finished with black pens, scanned, and applied over the pictures. The process was very instinctive and quick because of the tight deadline I had, but it was a fun project.

SARAH A. KING
WHISTLER, BRITISH COLUMBIA
WWW.SARAHAKING.COM

SARAH KING GREW UP IN LONDON, STUDIED GRAPHIC DESIGN AT THE UNIVERSITY OF BRIGHTON, AND CURRENTLY LIVES ON THE WEST COAST OF CANADA. SHE SPENDS AS MUCH TIME AS POSSIBLE IN THE MOUNTAINS SNOWBOARDING OR BY THE OCEAN SURFING AND SCUBA DIVING. HER WORK IS OFTEN INSPIRED BY HER SURROUNDINGS—NATURE, HISTORY, ADVENTURES, AND ANYTHING ELSE WEIRD AND WONDERFUL THAT FINDS ITS WAY ONTO PAPER.

HAND-PAINTED
RUSSIAN DOLLS

TELL US MORE ABOUT YOUR ART AND DESIGN BACKGROUND. ALSO, WHAT MADE YOU BECOME INTERESTED IN TYPOGRAPHY?

I was in a children's book club from age five to age ten. We wrote and illustrated short stories, made them into books, and sold them in local shops. It was a great introduction into the world of art and design and was the earliest influence I can remember that made me want to pursue illustration as a career. My father was a writer and my mother is an architect, and their support spurred my interest in graphic design and typography.

HOW DID YOU COME UP WITH YOUR STYLE?

I studied graphic design at the University of Brighton, where thirty graphic design students shared a studio with thirty illustration students. We were encouraged to work on projects with the illustrators, to learn from each other's techniques and ways of thinking. We also had access to some great tutors, as well as letterpress, book binding, and screenprinting workshops. While at Brighton, my work developed and finally came together in the style I have now.

SOME SAY THAT ANALOG AND DIGITAL DESIGN ARE TOTALLY OPPOSED, WHILE OTHERS BELIEVE THAT TECHNOLOGY AND TRADITIONAL ART CAN COEXIST. WHAT'S YOUR TAKE ON THIS?

I think analog and digital design can coexist; isn't there proof of that in so much of the work we see today? I definitely use both—hand drawing illustrations, scanning them, and editing them in Photoshop.

IS THERE ANY SPECIAL MATERIAL OR MEDIUM YOU WOULD LIKE TO USE FOR YOUR NEXT PROJECT?

I'd love to make some laser-etched skate decks. More painting would be great, too.

ABOVE:
TAKE CARE OF YOUR BIKE

LEFT
TYPOGRAPHIC MAPS,
SAN FRANCISCO MUSEUM
OF MODERN ART

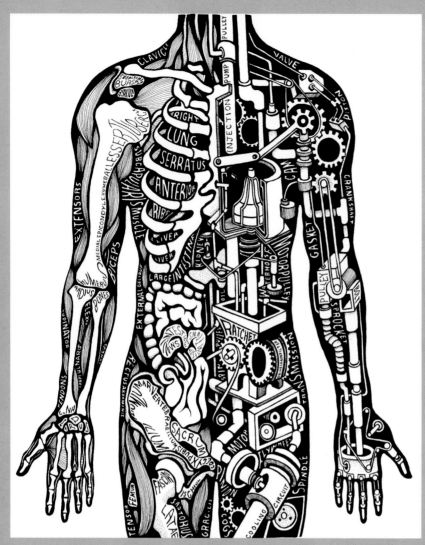

ABOVE
MEN AND MACHINES

ABOVE:
BIRD SKULL

I was moving around the country while working on this illustration. The brief was simply to create a machine man, so I took that directive as well as referencing medical drawings of the human form. I was driving from Cardiff to London with my brother at the time, and just outside Cardiff our car broke down. It took us around fifteen hours to get back to London, and with a lot of time spent in petrol stations (waiting for tow trucks), I did most of the work. I sketched out the torso, researched the human body and machine parts (the lungs are a washing machine), and did a rough sketch of how it could all fit together. The illustration was finished using pen and ink, gaps were filled in, and the machine part of the man was made to look like it could actually work.

JORDI RINS
BARCELONA
WWW.JORDIRINS.COM

JORDI RINS STUDIED GRAPHIC DESIGN AT THE ESCOLA MASSANA IN BARCELONA. HE WORKED AT TBWA BARCELONA AS AN ART DIRECTOR FOR BRANDS SUCH AS ADIDAS, NISSAN, CHUPA CHUPS, LEVI'S, AND MENTOS, AMONG OTHERS, AND IS NOW A FREELANCE ART DIRECTOR AND DESIGNER, WORKING FOR A RANGE OF CLIENTS.

When I have to make a mural, I look to classic lettering for reference. I then take pictures of the location and start testing compositions on my computer. I fill spaces as if it were the game Tetris, and when I get what I like, I show it to the client for approval. I project my drawing on the area and mark the letters. Then, I draw everything freehand, allowing for some human imperfections to give it an authentic look.

ABOVE/LEFT:
EL MASET MURAL

STEPH SAYS HELLO, STEPHANIE BAXTER

LEEDS, ENGLAND

WWW.STEPHSAYSHELLO.CO.UK

STEPH SAYS HELLO IS THE PORTFOLIO OF STEPHANIE BAXTER, A FREELANCE ILLUSTRATOR AND TYPOGRAPHER LIVING AND WORKING IN LEEDS, WEST YORKSHIRE. LIKE MOST ILLUSTRATORS, BAXTER IS HAPPIEST WITH A PENCIL, A PIECE OF PAPER, AND A HOT CUP OF TEA (MILK, NO SUGAR). SHE WORKS BOTH TRADITIONALLY WITH PEN, PAPER, AND INK, AS WELL AS DIGITALLY TO CREATE HER ILLUSTRATIONS AND HAND LETTERING.

RIGHT:
THE BEST SALAD
DRESSING

THE BEST SALAD DRESSING

Working with photography and hand lettering was a new experience for me with this piece, so my method may seem a little confused. First, I set up the photograph, which involved a lot of mess, balsamic vinegar, and trial and error! Then, after settling on a photograph I was happy with, I printed it and worked up the hand lettering on a piece of tracing paper. I then scanned the image into Photoshop and cleaned it up. I wanted to retain that hand-drawn element, so I didn't correct the image too much—I stuck to changing the levels and the contrast. I then used the paint bucket tool to add color (black in this case) to the lettering and deleted the background.

EAT SEASONALLY

SIGN-FIDELITY, CARL FREDRIK ANGELL

OSLO

WWW.SIGNFIDELITY.COM

CARL FREDRIK ANGELL, AKA FRISSO, IS A NORWEGIAN GRAPHIC DESIGNER WHOSE MAIN FOCUS IS ON HAND LETTERING AND SIGN PAINTING. WHILE ATTENDING KOLDING SCHOOL OF DESIGN IN DENMARK, HE WENT TO BOSTON FOR A THREE-MONTH APPRENTICESHIP WITH JOSH LUKE AND MEREDITH KASABIAN OF BEST DRESSED SIGNS, TO LEARN THE CRAFT OF SIGN PAINTING. HE IS USING WHAT HE LEARNED TO MAKE HIS MARK ON THE VISUAL LANDSCAPE OF OSLO BY BRINGING BACK HAND-PAINTED SIGNAGE.

ABOVE:
SKETCHBOOK
LETTERING

Working with gold leaf is a fun and challenging process that takes lots of repetition and practice to master. Reverse glass gilding requires planning out each step of the process before you start gilding.

One of the things I really enjoy about doing reverse glass is that you don't really get to see how it looks before it's finished. Seeing the amazing results is a major motivation to keep practicing and improving.

ABOVE:
US FLOOR RUSH

RIGHT:
HAND-DRAWN TYPEFACE

STUDIO AIRPORT

UTRECHT, NETHERLANDS

WWW.STUDIO-AIRPORT.NL

STUDIO AIRPORT IS VINCENT DE BOER, MAURITS WOUTERS, AND BRAM BROERSE. THEY WORK ON VARIOUS PROJECTS, SUCH AS IDENTITIES, FILMS, WEBSITES, BOOKS, POSTERS, CAMPAIGNS, AND TYPE.

We've been playing with calligraphy for about seven years, and we've had the ambition of ruling all different sorts of lettering, from script to black letter and Gothic to Roman. We practice with a lot of different pencils and brushes because with each pencil or brush there is a different way to make letters and forms. For the music poster series, the goal was to combine two ways of writing and keeping a balance between them. It was a challenge to have consistent white space on the posters. Selecting the musicians was a tough task as well!

run dmc krs-one africa bambaataa kool herc beastie boys eric b. rakim melle mel ll cool j grandmaster flash schoolly d bdp public enemy wu tang clan de la soul a tribe called quest big daddy kane nas ice cube biggie tupac nwa dr. dre snoopie gang starr pete rock cl smooth j dilla ice-t fugees cypress hill black moon buckshot artifacts redman epmd brand nubian gza large professor mobb deep jay-z oc ghostface jeru da damaja raekwon rza pharcyde m.o.p. masta ace big l dilla mos def smif n wessun common slick rick slumvillage lord finesse nate dogg busta rhymes edb method man

Y&G
BUENOS AIRES
WWW.BE.NET/YANIGUILLE

YANI ARABENA AND GUILLE VIZZARI WERE BORN IN BUENOS AIRES. THEY FIRST MET AT THE UNIVERSITY OF BUENOS AIRES, TEACHING AN ANNUAL TYPOGRAPHY COURSE. SINCE THEN, THEY'VE WORKED TOGETHER IN PROJECTS DIRECTLY RELATED TO TYPOGRAPHY, CALLIGRAPHY, AND ILLUSTRATION. THEY SURROUND THEMSELVES WITH INKS, COLORS AND TEXTURES, NIBS AND PENS, AND LETTERS AND ILLUSTRATIONS.

BELOW:
FLORA AND FAUNA ALPHABET

We came up with the idea to create three placemats—one for each meal of the day. We started sketching everything with pencils, pens, nibs, and ink. The final drawings were scanned, traced, retouched, and colored.

BELOW:
BZP BAZAAR TYPE
PLACEMATS

JACKSON ALVES
CURITIBA, BRAZIL
WWW.JACKSONALVES.COM

JACKSON ALVES IS A TYPOGRAPHER AND GRAPHIC DESIGNER IN BRAZIL WHOSE LOVE OF TRADITIONAL CALLIGRAPHY INFLUENCES HIS MODERN DESIGN PHILOSOPHY. ALVES CREATES CUSTOM TYPES AND LETTERING FOR DIFFERENT PROJECTS AND COMPANIES USING THE BASIC TENETS OF TRUE CALLIGRAPHY, AND THEN TRANSLATES THEM INTO DIGITAL WORKS OF ART.

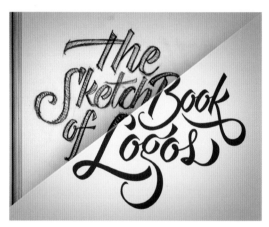

ABOVE: THE SKETCHBOOK OF LOGOS

ABOVE: CUSTOM TYPES SKETCH

OCUPA 15 MILHÕES
45% DE HABITANTES
DO TERRITÓRIO
27,5 1 médico
para 1090
IDADE MÉDIA 13 MILHÕES habitantes
DE HABITANTES
30,7 IDADE MÉDIA
1 médico para
cada 967 hab.
52 OCUPA
18,2%
MILHÕES DO
31 ANOS 1 médico
p/cada
IDADE MÉDIA 435 hab.
OCUPA 33,6
IDADE MÉDIA OCUPA TI-
DE HAB. TER-
MILHÕES 10,6% TO-
DO TERRITÓRIO
OCUPA 80 MILHÕES
18,8% DE HABITANTES
DO TERRI-
TÓRIO HABITANTES: 1 médico
p/ 412 hab.
27 MILHÕES
IDADE MÉDIA
33,7 1 médico
534 habitantes p/cada
OCUPA 6,8%
DO TERRITÓRIO

I mostly do calligraphy, but in this case, I started with straight lettering. The client was looking for a handmade typography map of Brazil, and I decided to do it with pencil and finish it with Nankin pen to do a "live trace" in Adobe Illustrator. But when I designed the first states of the map and vectorized it using live trace, it didn't look good because it had a lot of noise that the paper version didn't have. So I decided to design each letter in Illustrator, but instead of using the pen tool, I used the pencil tool and my tablet Wacom. It looks handmade because it has my real traces without noise from the live trace and the perfection of the pen tool. In the end, I added some texture to emulate something like wood type. I thought that it would be a fast project, but it took more time than I anticipated because I designed more than 500 characters by hand, without using the copy and paste command.

ABOVE/BELOW:
BRAZIL TYPOGRAPHIC
MAP FOR RAIA DROGASIL
GROUP'S MAGAZINE

EMMA DYSON
TAURANGA, NEW ZEALAND
WWW.BEHANCE.NET/EMMALEEDYSON

EMMA DYSON IS PASSIONATE ABOUT ALL THINGS VISUAL, INCLUDING TYPOGRAPHY, PAINTING, DRAWING, PHOTOGRAPHY, PRINT DESIGN, AND BRAND IDENTITY. SHE IS CONSTANTLY PUSHING THE BOUNDARIES TO DELIVER AN EFFECTIVE, FOCUSED, ORIGINAL, AND CREATIVE DESIGN THAT FITS THE CLIENT'S NEEDS AND GOALS.

I based my design for this package on something hand drawn as this would give an organic budget look to the products, but they would also be eye catching. Budget-conscious consumers need to find products fast and easily, with quantity being more important than the quality of the product. I sketched out lots of ideas and established the style, layout, and hierarchy of information. I then experimented with India ink and different brush sizes on A3 pieces of paper. When I had them looking almost perfect, I scanned them into the computer and replaced any words or letters that didn't look right with earlier experiments and played around with scale in Photoshop until I had a composition I was happy with. I would then bring that into Illustrator and live trace the typography and then apply color, etc. until I had the packaging design complete.

GINGER MONKEY
TOM LANE
BRISTOL, ENGLAND
WWW.GINGERMONKEYDESIGN.COM

TOM LANE, MORE COMMONLY KNOWN AS GINGER MONKEY, IS AN INDEPENDENT LETTERER, ILLUSTRATOR, AND DESIGNER. HIS DEEP EXPLORATION OF TECHNIQUES AND STYLES OF THE PAST ARE FUSED WITH TWENTY-FIRST-CENTURY SENSIBILITIES TO CREATE UNIQUE AND HIGHLY EMOTIVE IMAGES. LANE HAS WORKED EXTENSIVELY OVER THE LAST EIGHT YEARS FOR AN ARRAY OF INTERNATIONAL CLIENTS, LARGE AND SMALL, INCLUDING NIKE AIR JORDAN, COCA-COLA, SONY ERICSSON, BICYCLE, BMW, AND MERCEDES.

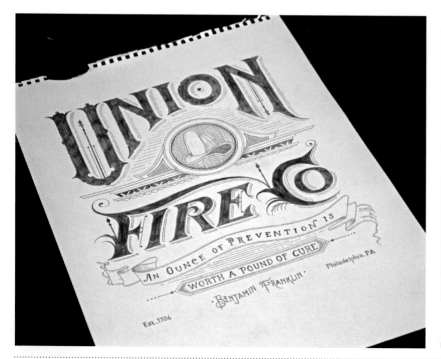

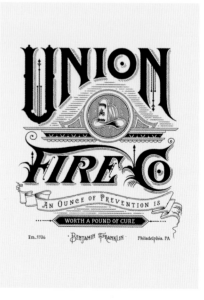

ABOVE/LEFT:
UNION FIRE CO. ARTWORK

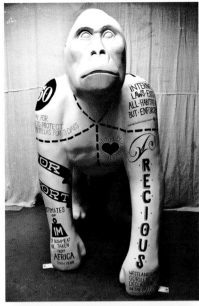

GOING GONE GORILLA

Setting about hand drawing type on a life-size plaster gorilla threw up some interesting challenges, but the process was ultimately very similar to drawing type on paper. That's once we became familiar with the rougher surface and the curves of the model. Due to time constraints, we chose to design and sketch the artwork on-site, on the gorilla. We used soft pencils to sketch the type; when we were happy with our outlines, we filled in using marker pens. The whole piece was cleaned up with a lot of rubbing out of the pencil lines with an eraser and some bits of white paint to cut back in where necessary. The model was then sprayed in a heat-sensitive black paint that, once warm, became translucent and revealed the artwork beneath.

HOM SWEET HOM, LAUREN HOM

NEW YORK CITY

WWW.HOMSWEETHOM.COM

LAUREN HOM IS A DESIGNER, ILLUSTRATOR, AND LETTERER. A RECENT GRADUATE OF THE SCHOOL OF VISUAL ARTS AND OWNER OF HOM SWEET HOM DESIGN STUDIO, SHE'S WORKED ON BRANDING, ILLUSTRATION, AND CUSTOM LETTERING FOR CLIENTS SUCH AS YOUTUBE, NESTLÉ, AND EVITE. A LOVER OF ALL THINGS CULINARY, TYPOGRAPHIC, AND HUMOROUS, SHE AIMS TO CREATE WORK THAT MAKES PEOPLE LAUGH OR FEEL HUNGRY. HER MOTTO IS, AND ALWAYS WILL BE, "WORK HARD, SNACK OFTEN."

LEFT:
I'LL SHAVE
MY LEGS
TOMORROW

ABOVE:
I'LL BE THERE IN
5 MINUTES

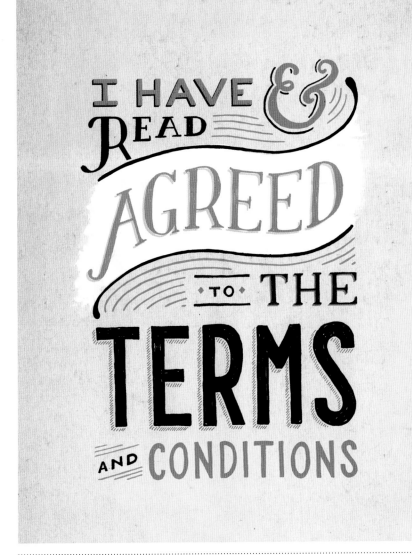

TERMS AND CONDITIONS

This Terms and Conditions poster is part of my Daily Dishonesty series, a project in which I letter and illustrate the little lies I encounter every day. My process is quite simple: I begin with a sharp pencil and my graph paper notebook. The grids really help me keep my shapes, curves, and spacing consistent. Once the pencil sketch is done, I take a fine black marker and ink the drawing. I scan it into the computer at a really high resolution, knock out the letters in black and white, and fine-tune everything on the computer—layout, coloring, and texturing. Though the majority of my process is digital, everything I produce always has a hand-done element to add a bit of my personality.

ANDY SMITH
HASTINGS, ENGLAND
WWW.ASMITHILLUSTRATION.COM

ANDY SMITH STUDIED ILLUSTRATION AT THE UNIVERSITY OF BRIGHTON AND THE ROYAL COLLEGE OF ART, LONDON. HIS WORK COMBINES ILLUSTRATION AND TYPOGRAPHY TO CREATE IMAGES THAT HAVE HUMOR, ENERGY, AND OPTIMISM, EXECUTED WITH A HANDMADE, HAND-PRINTED, TACTILE FEEL. AN ILLUSTRATOR FOR FOURTEEN YEARS, HE HAS A CLIENT LIST THAT INCLUDES NIKE, SONY PSP, ORANGE, *THE GUARDIAN*, MCDONALDS, CHANNEL 4, MERCEDES, AND PENGUIN BOOKS.

DO YOU HAVE ANY HEROES IN GRAPHIC DESIGN, TYPOGRAPHY, OR ILLUSTRATION?
In terms of influences, I think I've picked them up all over the place. Some have stuck with me and some I'm not keen on anymore, as I myself have developed and changed. People such as Stanley Spencer, Javier Mariscal, Chip Kidd, Art Chantry, Peter Blake, David Shrigley, and David Hockney all spring to mind.

WHAT ARE YOUR FAVORITE DESIGN TOOLS AND WHY?
My tools are fairly simple: pens and paper, Photoshop, and a screenprinting press. I like to silkscreen my work whenever possible.

ALL OF YOUR WORK HAS A VERY HANDMADE AESTHETIC. DO YOU DRAW EVERYTHING BY HAND FIRST?

I sketch everything out roughly on paper to begin with so I've got the basic structure with all the major words in there. Then, I'll scan that, and using a font on my computer — usually Helvetica — I'll place all the words where they are going to go to make sure it's a good composition and everything flows and is readable. Then, I'll print that out and use it as a template, drawing the type by hand.

HAND-RENDERED WORK IS BECOMING MORE AND MORE POPULAR. WHY DO YOU THINK THIS IS?

I think it's an inevitable reaction to the digital age, and it's just the same with illustration versus vectors, etc. Hand-drawn type has a lot of connotations that are popular with advertisers and brands — it's warm, honest, and authentic, and doesn't feel mass produced, as time has been taken to construct it. I really enjoy it as there's so much you can do with lettering, and every job is different, as a lot of the style is dictated by what the actual message is. I think of lettering not as words but as abstract shapes that I'm building a picture from.

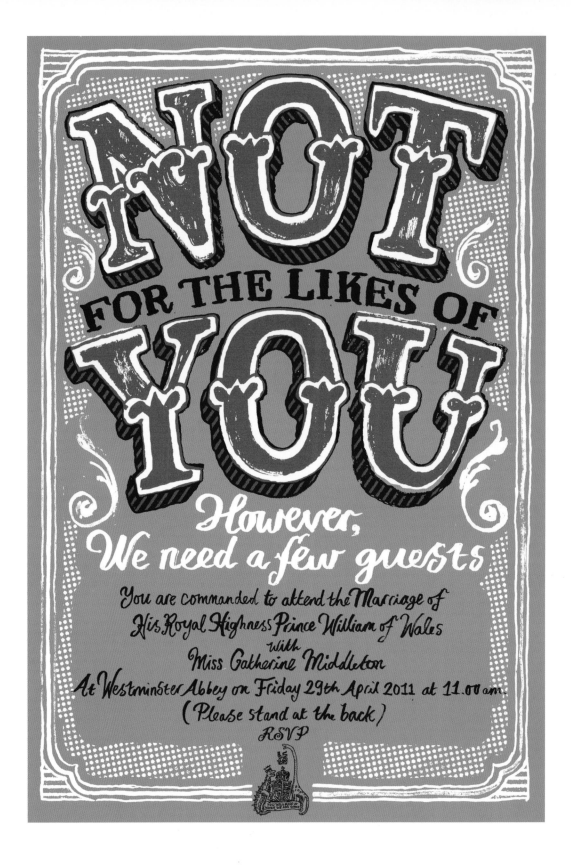

LONDON OLYMPICS

This was quite a complex illustration to work on, and it was especially difficult to provide a rough to my client as it needed to be built up bit by bit, and I couldn't really plan it beforehand—I just had to get started. I knew we were going to make a small map of London with as many sights as possible, so I began by sketching the buildings very roughly and placing them on the image around the Thames. The other main element would be the lettering from a long list of competing nations. I placed this on the map in Helvetica to figure out where everything would go. Once the layout was completed, I began again, this time drawing the buildings for real and then hand lettering all the names in as many styles as I could think of. The important thing was to get the final picture to balance so the viewer's eye is encouraged to move around the map and not settle on any particular point.

ABOVE:
LONDON
OLYMPICS

JEFF ROGERS

NEW YORK CITY

WWW.HOWDYJEFF.COM

JEFF ROGERS IS A MULTIDISCIPLINARY DESIGNER SPECIALIZING IN CUSTOM LETTERING, GRAPHIC DESIGN, AND ART DIRECTION. A PROUD TEXAS NATIVE, HE WORKS FROM HIS TINY STUDIO IN NEW YORK CITY ON PROJECTS FOR CLIENTS SUCH AS NIKE, GOOGLE, *THE NEW YORK TIMES*, MCDONALD'S, URBAN OUTFITTERS, AND MANY OTHERS. JEFF HAS RECEIVED AWARDS AND RECOGNITION FOR HIS DESIGN AND TYPOGRAPHY FROM THE TYPE DIRECTORS CLUB, COMMUNICATION ARTS, *PRINT* MAGAZINE, AND THE ONE SHOW.

FAR LEFT:
JERSEY
STRONG

LEFT:
DRUNKEN
PROMISES

OPPOSITE:
ACE HOTEL
MURAL

ACE HOTEL MURAL

I was asked by the Ace Hotel in New York City to create several large typographic murals to hang in various rooms. I wanted to focus on New York City–centered subject matter, and because the hotel places a large emphasis on music, I thought song lyrics about New York would be perfect. I sketched out a design for this David Bowie lyric in my large sketchpad, tweaked the design digitally, then projected the image on the canvas. I wanted to keep the design very simple with a limited color palette since I would be basically drawing out shapes on the raw canvas and filling in flat color, almost like a paint-by-number painting. In this case, something totally unique was created.

NATE WILLIAMS
SEATTLE
WWW.N8W.COM

NATE WILLIAMS, AKA ALEXANDER BLUE, IS AN ILLUSTRATOR WITH A LOVE FOR HAND LETTERING, CHILDREN'S ILLUSTRATION, AND NAÏVE ART. HE IS THE CREATOR OF ILLUSTRATOR MUNDO, LETTERPLAYGROUND, PROCONIST, AND THE CREACTIVISTS WEBSITES, AND IS CURRENTLY WRITING AND ILLUSTRATING SEVERAL HUMOROUS PICTURE BOOKS. HE VALUES CREATIVITY, CURIOSITY, PLAY, AND DISCOVERY, AND ENCOURAGES ASPIRING ILLUSTRATORS THROUGH CREATIVE EXERCISES, TALKS, AND WORKSHOPS.

For most of my work, it starts with brainstorming with a coffee on a park bench. I like to draw with pencil before I move to the computer because it's more spontaneous and I can sketch away from my studio. For this particular piece, the art director wanted a vintage-looking piece. So I thought of shapes the type could fit into and ways to emphasize the most important words. Once I had sentence shapes, I headed back to the studio and created it using a Wacom tablet. This allows for easy editing and usage.

CHAPTER 2
VINTAGE TWIST

TYPOGRAPHY THAT PAYS HOMAGE TO TIMES GONE BY IS EVER INCREASING IN POPULARITY. LOOKING BACK TO LOOK FORWARD IS A HUGE TREND, AND WITH GOOD REASON. THESE DESIGNERS HAVE A PASSION FOR VINTAGE TYPE, WHETHER RENDERED

DAN GRETTA

PHILADELPHIA

WWW.FOREFATHERSGROUP.COM

DAN GRETTA IS A DESIGNER ON THE EAST COAST WHO FOCUSES PRIMARILY ON BRANDING, ILLUSTRATION, AND TYPOGRAPHY. HE DOESN'T CATER TO ANY ONE STYLE, AS HE BELIEVES EACH PROJECT DESERVES ITS OWN. HE BELIEVES NO MEAL IS COMPLETE WITHOUT CHEESE, AND NO DAY COMPLETE WITHOUT COFFEE.

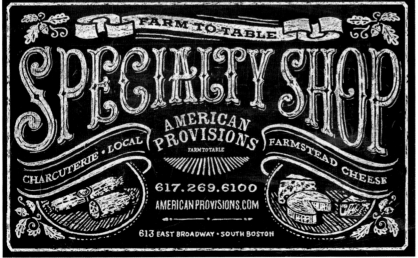

LEFT:
SPECIALTY
SHOP

ABOVE:
OWC SCRIPT
GRAPHIC T-SHIRT

NEIL BEECH

LONDON

NEIL BEECH IS A FREELANCE GRAPHIC DESIGNER AND ILLUSTRATOR WITH SIXTEEN YEARS, EXPERIENCE IN PRINT AND APPAREL. HIS SUCCESS LIES IN HIS ABILITY TO TREAT EVERY PROJECT AS IF IT WERE HIS FIRST, MAINTAINING THE SAME LEVEL OF FRESHNESS AND ENTHUSIASM.

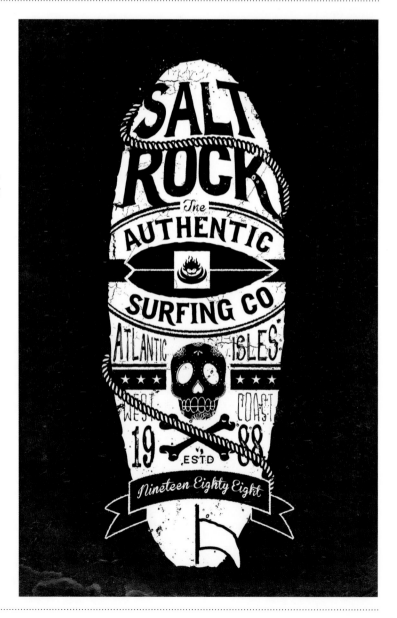

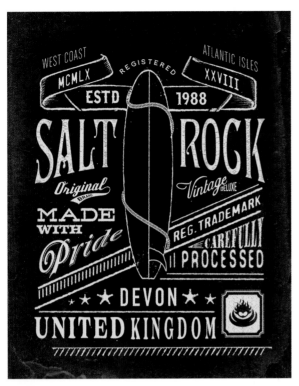

SALTROCK

When creating vintage-style designs, I literally surround myself with research. My office is wallpapered with printouts. I enjoy creating A–Zs of hand-drawn bespoke fonts that I can live trace and manipulate until I feel the design has all the right elements. When I am happy with the design, I will simply place bitmap textures over the piece to give it a certain vintage, aged effect.

OPPOSITE:
SALTROCK

XESTA STUDIO, HUGO MOURA

PORTO, PORTUGAL

WWW.XESTASTUDIO.COM

XESTA STUDIO IS A GRAPHIC DESIGN STUDIO BORN IN 2011. ITS MAIN FOCUS HAS BEEN TO INCLUDE SEVERAL STYLES AND TECHNIQUES OF CALLIGRAPHY, LETTERING, AND TYPOGRAPHY IN ITS WORKS AND TO EXPLORE SEVERAL TYPES OF MEDIA AND MATERIALS. WITH A BACKGROUND IN URBAN ART AND INFLUENCED BY ITS SURROUNDINGS, THE STUDIO SEEKS UNIQUE CREATIVE SOLUTIONS IN ALL ITS SERVICES.

BELOW:
TYPE SKETCHES

BELOW:
PLI MAGAZINE

WINLOVE WINE

The goal for this project was to create a more neutral image. We intentionally kept the design to only black and white. To distinguish the different regions and the type of wine, we drew different lettering for each bottle to create a coherent language by giving more emphasis to the general language of the product (each bottle has its own identity) than to the brand in question.

LEFT/BELOW:
WINLOVE WINE

JOEL FELIX
STOCKTON, CALIFORNIA
WWW.JOELFELIX.COM

JOEL FELIX IS A GRAPHIC DESIGNER, HAND LETTERER, AND TYPOGRAPHER WHO IS PASSIONATE ABOUT LETTERS AND ALL THINGS DESIGN. HE CAN OFTEN BE FOUND IN HIS ONE-MAN STUDIO SKETCHING OUT WORK FOR A WIDE VARIETY OF CLIENTS, INCLUDING JACK DANIEL'S, COACH, *DBUSINESS* MAGAZINE, BOTTLEROCK NAPA VALLEY, AND MANY MORE. FELIX SPECIALIZES IN LOGO AND IDENTITY WORK, WEB DESIGN, PACKAGING, HAND LETTERING, AND CUSTOM ILLUSTRATION. HIS WORK HAS BEEN FEATURED ON FPO (FOR PRINT ONLY, A DIVISION OF UNDERCONSIDERATION), WEB DESIGN LEDGER, *SMASHING* MAGAZINE, AND I HEART LOGOS.

RIGHT:
WINE CHALK

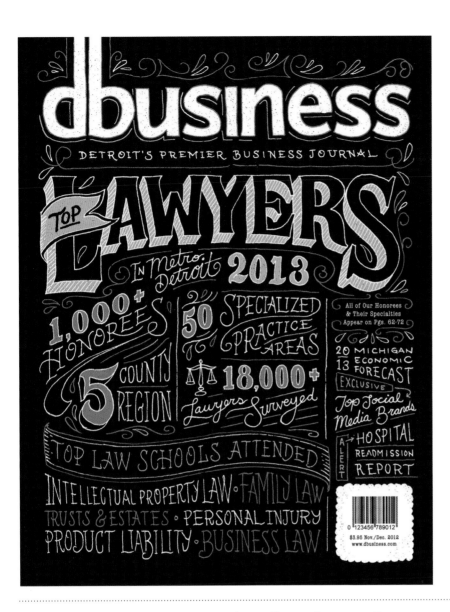

DBUSINESS COVER

You can begin to see hierarchy issues when it's all black and white. Color plays an important role in calling out information and creating a smooth flow of hierarchy. Once you've got the final inking scanned in (I usually scan in at high-res 600 dpi so I can blow it up and control the Illustrator tracing filter better), then you can clean things up in Illustrator. I switched places between the "18,000 Lawyers Surveyed" and the "50 Specialized Practice Areas." I felt the "18,000" was competing with the "2013" in the headline in the original pencil

drawing. Because this was now all vector, it was easy to group things and move them around a bit. I went through each headline and made refinements, some very minor, but it's always the small things that make the difference.

I worked closely with the art director at *DBusiness* on color options, and we ended up doing a three-color solution, which helped hierarchy. Something I learned in school, which you'd be smart to remember, is "White/paper is always another color." (Thanks, Gwen.) Especially when you're on a tight budget and can afford only a one- or two-color job, try and see how you can use the paper color to aid in your design.

ABOVE:
DBUSINESS JOURNAL
COVER

BEST DRESSED SIGNS
BOSTON
WWW.BESTDRESSEDSIGNS.COM

DEDICATED TO THE CRAFT OF HAND-PAINTED SIGNS, CUSTOM LETTERING, AND GOLD LEAF, BEST DRESSED SIGNS OFFERS CLIENTS THE BENEFIT OF QUALITY AND ATTRACTIVE HAND-CRAFTED SIGNAGE AND DESIGN. FOUNDERS JOSH LUKE AND MEREDITH KASABIAN ALSO PARTICIPATE IN GALLERY ART SHOWS, CONDUCT WORKSHOPS, AND GIVE LECTURES ON HISTORICAL ASPECTS OF THE SIGN-PAINTING TRADE.

NEVER AN OFF SEASON

For this particular project, we wanted the lettering design to interact with the deco architecture of Boston's Landmark Center, located across the street from the sign. The inspiration for the lettering and design came from early mid-century letterforms, which are juxtaposed with a vibrant color scheme to showcase Boston as a historical yet innovative city. Once the drawing was refined, a pattern was made by perforating large sheets of paper with tiny holes that followed the outline of the letters. We then placed the pattern paper on the wall in sections and pounced it with chalk, which goes through the perforated lines to give us a guideline for painting. To paint the sign, we brushed in the outlines and used rollers for the centers, and then went back and added the shadows and dimensions with large brushes. The whole sign is more than 6 feet (2 m) tall and 300 feet (91 m) long and took about a month to complete with just Josh Luke, Meredith Kasabian, and Carl Fredrik Angell working on it from a boom lift.

LEFT:
NEVER AN
OFF SEASON

TOP:
**ROME
SNOWBOARDS**

BOTTOM RIGHT:
**LINCOLN ARTS
PROJECT**

LEFT:
ALPHABET

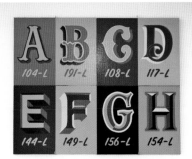

JILL DE HAAN
SALT LAKE CITY
WWW.JILLDEHAANART.PROSITE.COM

JILL DE HAAN IS A GRAPHIC DESIGNER SPECIALIZING IN FOLKSY DESIGN, PATTERNS, AND HAND LETTERING AND CALLIGRAPHY.

RIGHT:
ART HOUSE
CINEMA

UNION

You have known each other from the first glance of Aquaintance. To this point of commitment, AT SOME POINT YOU DECIDED TO MARRY. From that moment of Yes, to this moment of Yes, indeed, you have been making commitments in an informal way ALL OF THOSE conversations that were held in a car, or over a meal, or during long walks - all those conversations that began with "I WILL" "When we're married," and "WE WILL" - all those late night talks - and continued with and, "YOU WILL" and "WE WILL" - all those late night talks - and all that included "someday," and "somehow" and "maybe," - and these those promises, that are unspoken matters of the heart, all these common things, and more are THE REAL PROCESS OF A Wedding

THE SYMBOLIC VOWS that you are about to make are a way of saying to one another, "You know all those things that we've PROMISED, and HOPED, and DREAMED Well I meant it all, EVERY WORD LOOK AT ONE ANOTHER and remember this moment in time. BEFORE THIS MOMENT you have been many things to one another - aquaintance, friend, companion, lover, dance partner, even teacher for you have learned so much from one another these past few years. Shortly, you shall say a few words that will take you across a threshold of life, and things between you will never quite be the same. For after today you shall say to the world This is my HUSBAND, this is my WIFE.

BY ROBERT FULGHUM

BELOW:
RUTH'S
FRENCH
BREAD

UNION
For my Posterama Union piece, I started with a small sketch to figure out where I wanted the line breaks to be. I then scanned in my sketch and increased it to the size that I wanted the final piece of artwork to be (about 11 X 17 inches, or 28 X 43 cm). From there, I attached the printout to my Lightpad to use as a guide and carefully redrew the entire piece at the larger, more detailed size. The client requested that the quote be written in pencil to give it more of an organic feel, and I really like the effect the pencil gave the project. After drawing it up, I then scanned in the final penciled piece and made some small adjustments in Photoshop.

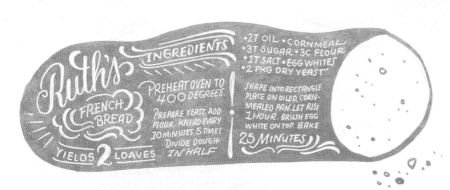

Ruth's FRENCH BREAD
INGREDIENTS
•2T OIL •CORNMEAL
•3T SUGAR •3C FLOUR
•1T SALT •EGG WHITES
•2 PKG DRY YEAST

PREHEAT OVEN TO 400 DEGREES
PREPARE YEAST. ADD FLOUR. KNEAD EVERY 10 MINUTES, 5 TIMES. DIVIDE DOUGH IN HALF

SHAPE INTO RECTANGLE PLACE ON OILED, CORN-MEALED PAN. LET RISE 1 HOUR. BRUSH EGG WHITE ON TOP. BAKE 25 MINUTES

YIELDS 2 LOAVES

Enjoy!

JON CONTINO
NEW YORK CITY
WWW.JONCONTINO.COM

NEW YORK NATIVE JON CONTINO IS AT THE FOREFRONT OF TODAY'S MOST INFLUENTIAL DESIGNERS. HIS UNIQUE STYLISTIC APPROACH BLENDS OLD WORLD WHIMSY WITH A MODERN, MINIMALISTIC SENSIBILITY THAT CREATES A DISTINCT PERSONALITY, IMITATED TIME AND TIME AGAIN. CONTINO'S DEDICATED EFFORTS CONTINUE TO BLUR BOUNDARIES AND AFFECT MODERN TRENDS IN ALL FACETS OF THE CREATIVE INDUSTRY.

LEFT:
DOCKERS
SKETCHES

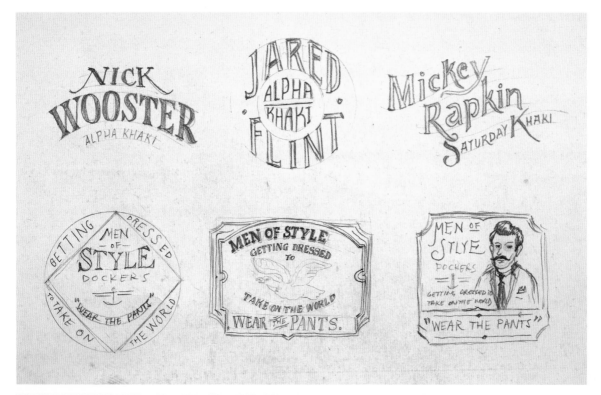

WHAT IS YOUR ART AND DESIGN BACKGROUND, AND WHAT MADE YOU BECOME INTERESTED IN TYPOGRAPHY?

I've been drawing since the day I could hold a pencil. My family was not only supportive of my interest in drawing but also fairly creative themselves. My mother is an artist, my father is a carpenter, and my grandmother nurtured every inkling of interest I had in illustration and lettering. I spent my childhood drawing logos and letters as much as possible. When I got older, I became more interested in graffiti and T-shirt graphics, and that was sort of like my second wind as a childhood artist. In my early teens, I played in a bunch of hardcore bands all over New York, and that pretty much opened the floodgates for me: merchandise, record layouts, flyers, websites. I did it all and quickly started a part-time career as a graphic designer in 1997. By 2005, I was running my own studio and trying to focus all of my efforts on creating beautiful typography and illustration for whatever client I could convince to use it. As time went on, I honed my skills into the designer I am today.

YOU SEEM TO USE BRUSHES A LOT IN YOUR WORK; WHAT MAKES USING THEM SO APPEALING TO YOU?

The brush stroke is the most beautiful mark an artist can make, in my opinion. Thins to thicks and rogue marks terminating the line create an incredible image that you just can't duplicate any other way. I like to be able to utilize those shapes and marks in lettering to give it a strong sense of personality; after all, personality is the root of what makes something appealing.

DO YOU HAVE ANY HEROES IN GRAPHIC DESIGN, TYPOGRAPHY, OR ILLUSTRATION?

All of my primary heroes in anything are the family members I mentioned, but if we're talking public figures, then I'd have to say my top three most inspiring people are Ralph Steadman, Herb Lubalin, and Kimou Meyer. I feel as though the body of work from those three guys has given me endless amounts of joy and will continue to do so for as long as I can imagine.

OPPOSITE/BELOW:
LOUIE LETTERING

OPPOSITE:
JACK DANIEL'S
DECLARATIONS
OF INDEPENDENCE
CAMPAIGN

JACK DANIEL'S DECLARATIONS OF INDEPENDENCE CAMPAIGN

After doing a handful of sketches, I designed the shape of the anvil as the basis for the design. I then burned a negative version onto a screen and printed its background onto a sheet of heavy duty watercolor paper stock. That gave me the opportunity to use india ink and watercolor as my preferred medium within the shape of the anvil and white paint markers to highlight portions of the black with lettering, decorative elements, and the Jack Daniel's logo. It was a process that involved jumping in and out of different media.

The original idea for the project was to tattoo the entire piece on an animal hide exactly as you see it. Unfortunately, because of time constraints, I had to figure out an alternate process, and that ended up being the combination of screen printing and brush lettering. If I had had an extra week, I definitely would have set up a piece of leather and my tattoo machine and done it entirely that way. I'm really itching to do it someday.

BELOW:
ORIGINAL
MAKERS CLUB

SEB LESTER
LEWES, ENGLAND
WWW.SEBLESTER.CO.UK

TRAINED IN GRAPHIC DESIGN AT CENTRAL SAINT MARTINS, SEB LESTER WORKS AS A TYPE DESIGNER, ILLUSTRATOR, AND ARTIST. HE HAS CREATED TYPEFACES AND TYPE ILLUSTRATIONS FOR SOME OF THE WORLD'S BIGGEST COMPANIES, PUBLICATIONS, AND EVENTS, INCLUDING APPLE, NIKE, INTEL, *THE NEW YORK TIMES*, THE 2010 VANCOUVER WINTER OLYMPICS, AND J. D. SALINGER'S FINAL REISSUE OF *THE CATCHER IN THE RYE*. AS A SENIOR TYPE DESIGNER AT MONOTYPE IMAGING FOR NINE YEARS, HE DEVELOPED CUSTOM TYPEFACES FOR CLIENTS INCLUDING BRITISH AIRWAYS, WAITROSE, *THE DAILY TELEGRAPH*, H&M, AND BARCLAYS.

MIGHTIER

I wanted to produce a piece of expressive lettering that illustrated this timeless adage. It's a dramatic composition of complementary calligraphic styles developed especially for this piece. It's influenced by eighteenth-century calligraphy and twentieth-century sign writing, but with some very modern touches. I started with sketchbook drawings, which I scanned in, converted to vectors in Illustrator, and then cleaned up and embellished in FontLab.

LEFT:
MIGHTIER

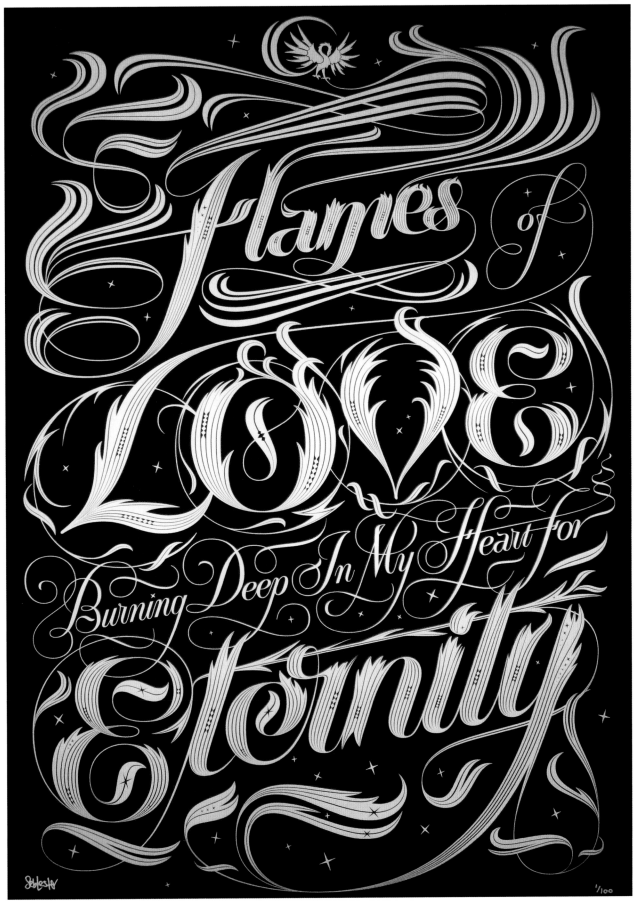

COFFEE MADE ME DO IT, SIMON ÅLANDER

STOCKHOLM

WWW.COFFEEMADEMEDOIT.COM

SIMON ÅLANDER IS THE FACE BEHIND COFFEE MADE ME DO IT, BASED IN SWEDEN. HE IS PASSIONATE ABOUT TYPOGRAPHY AND LETTERING AND EXPERIMENTING WITH DIFFERENT TECHNIQUES—BOTH ANALOG AND DIGITAL. HE IS INSPIRED BY FOOD, MUSIC, STREET WEAR, AND THE SNEAKER CULTURE. HE ALSO LIKES COFFEE (A LOT).

THE EMPIRE STATE NEW YORK
This piece started out as a rough sketch during a casual sketch session. A couple of months later, I found the sketch and thought it was too nice to be thrown away. So I spent a couple of hours refining it and I also added the "The Empire State" part. I scanned it and made a few adjustments in Photoshop before I imported it into Illustrator for vectorization.

BELOW:
THE EMPIRE STATE
NEW YORK

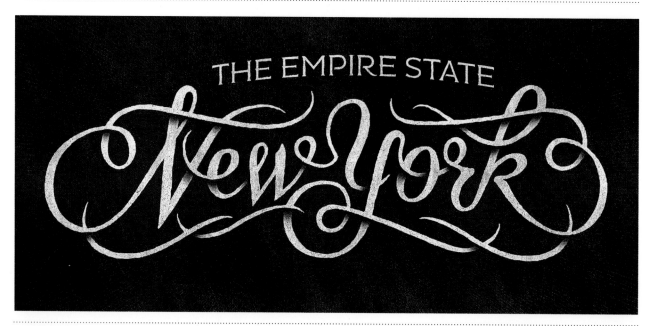

OZAN KARAKOC
LOS ANGELES
WWW.OZANKARAKOC.COM

GRAPHIC DESIGNER OZAN KARAKOC WAS BORN IN ISTANBUL, TURKEY, BUT NOW LIVES AND WORKS IN LOS ANGELES. HE IS THE FOUNDER OF THE WORLD FAMOUS, AWARD-WINNING ONLINE ART MAGAZINE *BAK*. AS A MULTIDISCIPLINARY DESIGNER, KARAKOC CREATES TYPOGRAPHIC PIECES, MOVIE AND TELEVISION SHOW POSTERS, MAGAZINE LAYOUTS, WEBSITES, AND 360-DEGREE ADVERTISING CAMPAIGNS.

MUSTAFA KEMAL ATATURK QUOTES

Ataturk Quotes Project is an homage to Mustafa Kemal Ataturk, who is one of the most visionary leaders of all time and the founder of the modern Turkish Republic. I put together six of his inspirational sayings and turned them into typographic compositions. First, I started drawing the layouts on a sketchbook with a pencil and markers. Then I re-created them digitally. Each poster has a different background.

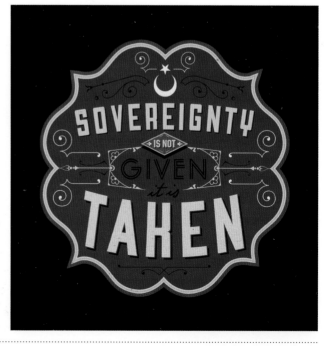

ABOVE/RIGHT:
MUSTAFA KEMAL ATATURK QUOTES

TOMASZ BIERNAT
SEATTLE
WWW.TOMASZBIERNAT.US

BORN IN THE 1970S IN WARSAW, TOMASZ BIERNAT IS PART OF THE NEW GENERATION OF POLISH GRAPHIC DESIGNERS. THROUGH YEARS OF SELF-DIRECTED LEARNING, HE HAS SPECIALIZED IN MANY DIFFERENT AREAS, SUCH AS BRANDING, TYPOGRAPHY, CAR DESIGN, CHINESE ARTWORK, GUILLOCHE, CRAYON DRAWINGS, AND T-SHIRT DESIGN.

LEFT:
FOR WE WALK

RIGHT:
100% OF NMC

MARTIN SCHMETZER

STOCKHOLM

WWW.MARTINSCHMETZER.COM

MARTIN SCHMETZER IS A DESIGNER WHO FOCUSES ON HAND-DRAWN TYPOGRAPHY WITH A HIGH LEVEL OF DETAIL. HE STARTED HIS OWN BUSINESS TWO YEARS AGO, AND THANKS TO THE INTERNET AND DESIGN BLOGS, HE HAS GOTTEN WORK AND GAINED PROMINENCE FOR HIS TYPE DESIGN.

WESC T-SHIRT GRAPHIC SKETCH
I always start with pen on paper before turning to the computer. After a couple of rough sketches to explore different compositions and solutions for WeSC to consider, I redrew the approved design tightly with much more detail. After that, I scanned and started vectorizing in Illustrator. A little funny fact is that I drew the whole vector illustration using only the touchpad on my MacBook Pro.

RIGHT:
WESC T-SHIRT
GRAPHIC SKETCH

TOP LEFT:
PUNK'N
BREWSTER
SKETCH

LEFT:
THE
BROWNSTONE
BREWING CO.
SKETCH

ABOVE:
THE BREW HOUSE
SKETCH

BELOW:
HOW TO DO
EVERYTHING
BETTER IN 2013,
MEN'S HEALTH
MAGAZINE

JASON CARNE
NEPTUNE CITY, NEW JERSEY
WWW.JASONCARNE.COM

JASON CARNE IS A TWENTY-FIVE-YEAR-OLD HAND-LETTERING AFICIONADO AND ANTIQUARIAN JUNK COLLECTOR EXTRAORDINAIRE FROM NEPTUNE CITY, NEW JERSEY. HE HAS AN EXTENSIVE MUSIC COLLECTION AND AN EVER-GROWING LIBRARY OF SIGN-PAINTING AND LETTERING BOOKS AND IS A CONNOISSEUR OF SCREEN-PRINTED POSTERS AND AN AVID ANIMAL AND TRAVEL ENTHUSIAST.

PLEASE TELL US ABOUT YOUR ART AND DESIGN BACKGROUND.

To be honest, my design background is basically nonexistent. I've never had any formal education on design or typography. I'm 100 percent self-taught, and it shows, but I like that in a way. The minor imperfections and the slight inconsistencies in my letterforms give my work a bit of character it may not have otherwise had if I adhered to some sort of strict code or guideline from a set of classes. From a very young age, I thoroughly enjoyed illustration and coloring, but the interest in lettering and typography didn't surface until after my short stint in college. I was only in school for a single semester back in 2006 at the Wentworth Institute of Technology in Boston, for architectural engineering, before leaving when my mother passed away. On the heels of that terrible situation, I decided to leave school and stay home. During that low period, I revisited my first love of art and design and began designing for local bands and independent record labels.

LEFT:
FANTASTIC SIGNS

I always had an obsession with heavy-metal band logos, which is where I think my love for lettering began, although it wasn't readily apparent to me at first that it was those very logos where my love of letterforms came from. On some level, I always had an understanding, albeit an undeveloped one, that a band's logo was its cornerstone, its face, and visual voice. The hallmark of a good band logo was if I knew what they sounded like before even putting the record on, and that notion carried over into the business world as my career grew and developed.

As time went on, my lettering style shifted multiple times until I arrived at the last stop in the train station, which was that of the late 1800s and early 1900s. Instantly,

I connected on a very strong level with the attention to detail and high level of craftsmanship of the antique advertising and ephemera. The pride and discipline that shone through the work of those artisans was unlike anything I'd ever seen, and I wanted desperately to revive that authenticity and genuine love for the craft of lettering in advertising. What I really loved was that each project had a completely unique and custom approach; it didn't feel like the modern assembly line-style of advertising we're visually barraged with daily. While extremely ornate in nature, there was tact, class, and restraint shown with many pieces that were tailored specifically for the business they were intended for.

BELOW:
TRIBE MURAL

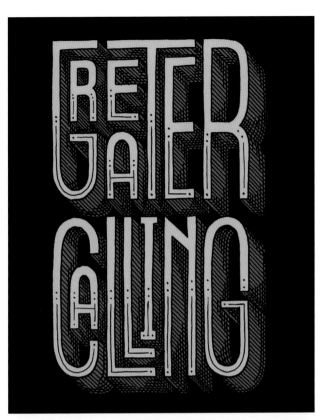

A LOT OF YOUR WORK IS CREATED BY HAND; DO YOU ALWAYS TRY TO WORK THIS WAY? WHAT IS THE APPEAL?

Yes, all my work is done by hand without exception, in at least one phase. I'm always reluctant to take on a project if it doesn't allow me to work by hand in some capacity or create something completely custom. To me, custom is king, and the appeal lies within the fact that I offer something that is a one-of-a-kind product to a client that no one else will ever have. I'm not interested in creating with premade fonts or typefaces; it's just not my style and not something I'm passionate about, and without passion, what's the point? I acknowledge the necessity for that sort of design and respect those who can do it well, but it just doesn't resonate as strongly with me as creating something completely unique does.

LEFT:
SEVENLY CHARITY
GRAPHICS

BELOW:
HALFCUT

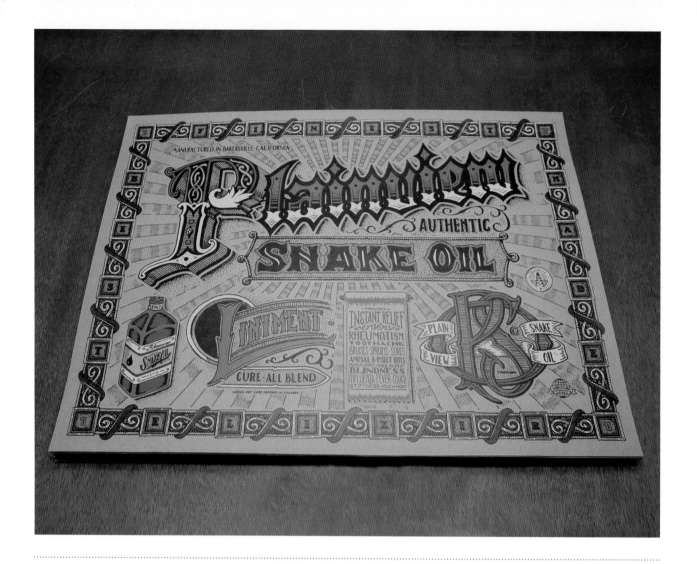

WHAT HAS BEEN YOUR FAVORITE TYPOGRAPHY PROJECT TO DATE AND WHY?

The Plainview Snake Oil poster is easily my favorite project I've done thus far. Daniel Day-Lewis is consistently one of the finest actors in Hollywood. In "There Will Be Blood," his character, Daniel Plainview, is a ruthless, cutthroat oil tycoon who is a bit of a metaphorical snake-oil salesman. Instead of selling a cure-all liniment, he's selling the promise of salvation to a wasteland of a town named Bakersville in California. However, as with any snake-oil story, it's soon apparent that his cure-all remedy he's boasted is just a bunch lies wrapped in a fancy package. There are a ton of nods to the film within the poster, which those who've seen the movie will surely get (maybe you'll even learn a few things you didn't know about the movie).

WHAT WOULD YOUR DREAM PROJECT BE?

This is a question that I could answer so many different ways, but the one project that I always come back to is painting a large-scale mural or advertisement on the side of an old brick building. The hand-painted advertisement, especially in long-standing urban areas with a high degree of visibility, is the holy grail for me. Coming across something like that is a rarity nowadays. It's the equivalent of seeing an endangered species in the wild—they're out there, but you really have to do some searching. There are a few people doing it rather well and keeping it alive, such as the team at Colossal Media, but not in that early 1900s style I'm drawn to. Ideally, it would be for a record store, bookshop, or a travel agency, but it could really be for anything so long as I like the business.

FRANCIONI, TAYLOR & LOPEZ

The funeral business is a dreary one; I would know, seeing as I actually live above the funeral home this piece was designed for! If ever there was an industry in dire need of a facelift or just a bit of life injected into it, this would be it. The Francioni, Taylor & Lopez Funeral Home has been in business since 1881, making it easily one of the oldest buildings in the area, as well as one of the longest-running businesses, but their advertising when they hired me didn't reflect that heritage and longevity. The previous advertisement had a few pieces of clip art tossed together with some cliché type choices. It was a passable advertisement, but it didn't have character, it lacked authenticity, and it just blended into the page with the all of the other advertisements from the other funeral homes in the obituary section. My main obstacle to overcome in this design was keeping all of the copy of the original advertisement and then arranging it in an aesthetically pleasing way, all while keeping it no larger than your standard business card. As you can see, it's a lot of lettering for a small area, and balancing design with legibility and sensible hierarchy was rather difficult. Though challenging, the end result was well worth the effort, as they now have a piece that boldly stands out from the rest without being too heavy-handed and speaks to their historic business, building, and tradition.

BELOW:
FRANCIONI,
TAYLOR &
LOPEZ

AARON VON FRETER
COLUMBUS, OHIO
WWW.BEHANCE.NET/VONFRETER

AARON VON FRETER WAS BORN AND RAISED IN COLUMBUS, OHIO, BUT IN 2000, HE MOVED TO EUROPE TO PURSUE HIS CAREER AS A GRAPHIC DESIGNER. VON FRETER HAS BEEN DOING DESIGN WORK IN THE CLOTHING INDUSTRY FOR THE PAST TWELVE YEARS.

BELOW/RIGHT:
HAND MADE

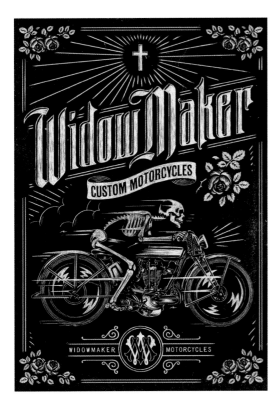

WIDOW MAKER

I wanted to capture the story of the Widow Maker through my design. It was a nickname given to the Kawasaki H3 Mach IV motorcycle in the 1970s because of its dangerous handling. For me, this project was like working with several pieces of a puzzle. I drew a lot of elements, researched vintage typography, and then drew the Widow Maker font. Once I was happy with the design, I redrew the entire piece very roughly to achieve a different aesthetic. When I was about 80 percent complete with the project, I found out that there was a motorcycle company based in the USA calling themselves Widow Maker, so I contacted the owner and asked if he would be interested in purchasing the design. For me, this piece was special because the design actually found its way home. It's exactly where it belongs, and I can't think of anything more gratifying as an artist.

BELOW:
VAUGHN ORIGINAL
SWING TAGS

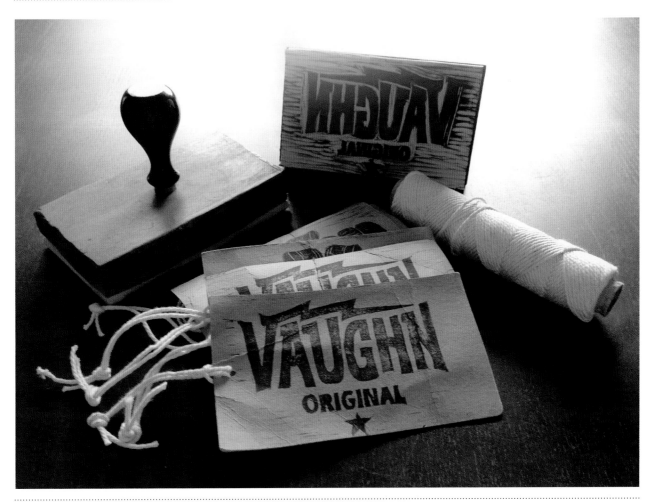

SIMON WALKER

AUSTIN, TEXAS

WWW.SIMONWALKERTYPE.COM

SIMON WALKER IS A GRAPHIC DESIGNER CURRENTLY WORKING IN THE DESIGN DEPARTMENT AT GSD&M IN AUSTIN. HE DOES A LOT OF FREELANCE WORK IN HIS FREE TIME, WHICH MAKES UP MOST OF WHAT YOU SEE OF HIS WORK ONLINE.

BELOW, CLOCKWISE FROM TOP LEFT

A BIT OF CRUMPET

CIDER LOGO

ORDER HERE

NAUGHTY NICETIES

TEA PARLOUR

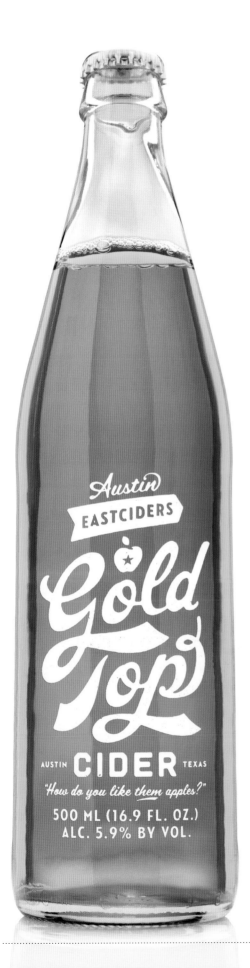

GOLD TOP CIDER LABELS

For the Gold Top label, I was asked to pursue a look that had a classic Austin feel to it—something vintage and Texas-feeling but with a bright playfulness to complement the style of cider. I pulled out all the tricks for this label: custom script for Austin, a more industrial custom typeface for the Gold Top lettering, a Texas star, the Texas state shape, ribbon all wrapped up in a tall badge shape to complement the bottle on which it would be placed. It might have actually been produced this way had we not discovered a website showcasing genuine vintage bottles with silk-screened lettering on them. The client went away and crunched some numbers, and before long, the existing bottle design featuring one-color script type printed directly on the bottle was finished and on the shelves.

GEORGIA HILL

BERLIN

WWW.GEORGIAHILL.TUMBLR.COM

GEORGIA HILL IS AN AUSTRALIAN FREELANCE TYPOGRAPHER, ILLUSTRATOR, AND GRAPHIC DESIGNER WORKING IN BERLIN. HAVING COMPLETED HER BACHELOR OF VISUAL COMMUNICATION DEGREE AT THE UNIVERSITY OF TECHNOLOGY IN SYDNEY, AUSTRALIA, SHE HAS BEEN STEADILY FREELANCING AND WORKING ON A RANGE OF PERSONAL AND AGENCY PROJECTS WITH HER ORIGINAL, HAND-GENERATED TYPOGRAPHIC TREATMENTS.

BELOW:
AFTER THE DARK

BELOW:
WORLD BAR POSTERS

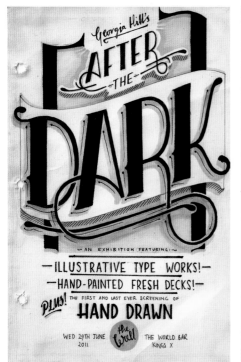

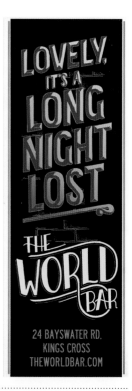

BELOW:
THE DENIAL OF
PLEASURE

TYPOGRAPHIC DECK COLLECTION

My type work usually starts with the phrasing and then looking at other limits—in this case, knowing I have three main colors and three decks to fill as a strong set. From here, I sketch up loose typographic styles and layouts side by side, which usually tighten up quickly. With this project, I skipped doing any transfers, rather sketched the final art directly onto the decks and got down to painting. It can be great with client work to keep things digital and easy to change, but I love coming at personal projects like this and letting the details and feeling build up as I work rather than planning them out.

NO ENTRY DESIGN

NEW YORK CITY

WWW.NOENTRYDESIGN.COM

NO ENTRY DESIGN IS THE ALIAS OF A GRAFFITI ARTIST WHO WANTED TO START MAKING A LIVING DOING DESIGN. THE FOUNDER, NEV, IS A MULTIDISCIPLINARY ARTIST WHO HAS A BACKGROUND WORKING AS A SCENIC ARTIST IN THE FILM PRODUCTION INDUSTRY. AFTER MOVING TO NEW YORK CITY, HE FOUND A PASSION FOR BRANDING SMALL START-UP RESTAURANTS AND SMALL BUSINESSES. IN THE LAST FEW YEARS, HE HAS BEEN ACTIVELY PURSUING THAT PASSION AND RAPIDLY DEVELOPING HIS SKILLS AS A DESIGNER, SIGN PAINTER, AND PHOTOGRAPHER.

PLEASE TELL US ABOUT YOUR ART AND DESIGN BACKGROUND.

I grew up in the graffiti community. To sum it up, that world is the polar opposite of the commercial art world, so it's been a very rough transition for me to establish myself as a designer. My interest in typography grew organically, as painting graffiti art is essentially the art of manipulating letters. The funny thing about it is that when I paint graffiti lettering, I am less concerned with the legibility of the letters and more concerned with how they flow into each other. The harder to read, the better it is! When I am doing type work, it is all about structure, and it's a good challenge to me in the sense that it's the opposite process from my style of graffiti work. My upbringing in graffiti trained me to produce clean lines in one quick stroke; having that skill helped me a lot with my hand-painted typography work. A few years ago, I really started to notice a lot of the hand-painted signage on locally owned businesses around New York, so I started paying a lot of attention to the intricate type work of good alcohol labels. From there, I started merging those styles into my personal artwork, and it eventually started influencing my design style.

WHAT DRIVES YOU TO PAINT SO MUCH BY HAND?

My motto is "work hard, not smart." I grew up creating art without the budget to get my work produced, and I've taken that same work ethic into the design projects that I genuinely take pride in. The work I've done for bigger agencies never really was anything I took that much pride in, so I usually don't bother to show it off.

WHAT DO YOU THINK IS IMPORTANT ABOUT SKETCHING OUT A DESIGN BEFORE USING THE COMPUTER?

When it comes to creating a logo, I feel it's definitely important because it makes the mark customized and original. Any generic designer can pick out a font and make a quick logo, but not any designer can draw a custom logo from scratch. The only issue with working this way is that my clients have no idea how much work actually goes into it.

SWALLOW CAFE

Swallow Cafe is a little coffee spot in Brooklyn that I frequent. Everyone who worked there knew me as the dude who was always drawing things and painting walls around the neighborhood. They had recently switched ownership and changed the name of the café, but they still had the old sign outside. So, I was chatting with one of the guys who worked there and told him they needed a logo and a new sign. From there,

I drew up some type and put a bird on it. At the time, I was still doing a lot of work constructing movie sets, so I used the tools I had available at the shop I worked at and built a nice wooden sign that I painted in the corner of my apartment. Because of the abundance of art in the neighborhood it's located in, it seemed fitting to hook up a mural on the building to help it stand out. So, I put a bird on it.

ABOVE:
SWALLOW CAFE

CHAPTER 3
PLAYFUL TYPE

USING ILLUSTRATION, PATTERNS, AND SELF-MADE
RULES, THESE DESIGNERS AND ILLUSTRATORS CREATE
PLAYFUL TYPE. THEY LET TASTE, VISION, AND MESSAGE
TAKE CONTROL.

PAUL THURLBY
LONDON
WWW.PAULTHURLBY.COM

PAUL THURLBY HAS BUILT UP AN IMPRESSIVE LIST OF COMMISSIONS, WORKING FOR CLIENTS INCLUDING *THE NEW YORKER*, *THE GUARDIAN*, TATE ENTERPRISES, THE FRENCH TOURIST BOARD, AND OTHERS. HIS STYLE HAS BEEN DESCRIBED AS RETRO-MODERN. THE AESTHETICS ARE RETRO AND THE SUBJECT MATTER IS MODERN. HE USES OLD BOOKS, POSTCARDS, AND PIECES OF PAPER FOR THE BACKGROUNDS OF HIS ILLUSTRATIONS; THIS SOMETIMES INVOLVES BUYING AN OLD BOOK FROM A CHARITY SHOP JUST TO USE ITS BACK COVER.

ALPHABET LETTERS

As with all the other alphabet letters I work on, I start by looking through my dictionary for words that I could transform into their initial letter. When the word is decided, I sketch out ideas and work up a basic composition in my sketchbook. Then, I transfer it to layout paper and draw over and over again to get things just right. After that, I scan the elements into Photoshop, along with various found textures and backgrounds. Color would be decided in Photoshop after some experimentation.

DANIELLE IS HERE
LAWTON, OKLAHOMA
WWW.DANIELLEISHERE.COM

DANIELLE DAVIS HAS A GREAT LOVE FOR LETTERING AND ILLUSTRATION WITH
A FOCUS ON LETTERFORMS. SHE ALWAYS STRIVES TO BETTER HER SKILLS
WITH EACH NEW PROJECT AND ENJOYS EXPLORING THE CRAZY AND AMAZING
LENGTHS THAT LETTERING CAN GO TO. SHE HAS WORKED WITH CLIENTS SUCH AS
NICKELODEON AND VSA PARTNERS AND IS EXCITED FOR WHATEVER THE FUTURE
DECIDES TO THROW HER WAY.

FAR LEFT:
LET'S BE REAL

LEFT:
LET US MAKE YOUR
NEXT EVENT COOL

HAND LETTERING FOR *THE GUARDIAN*

Depending on the needs of the project, I can tackle the brief from the project's art director in a few ways. If the lettering needs to be more structured and flowing, perhaps for an ad that needs to scream "classy," I'll letter a few key words from the approved headlines in two to three different styles from which a few rounds of client feedback will help me hone into the style that best works. I work all digitally because I'm not so hot on the pencil sketching. I actually work best with my mouse and Adobe Illustrator to create any roughs that then get cleaned up and tweaked for final output. Then it's steamroll ahead to the finished lettering.

For this particular title lettering for *The Guardian* newspaper, however, I was able to work on the brief from the complete opposite approach. The client gave me free reign, but it needed to be bold colors and more of a casual feel that would catch the eye of a younger audience. I was given a copy of the article in order to help spark ideas for any illustrated imagery that could help enhance the title lettering. After some minor tweaking from the art director's feedback, it was approved and was rushed to print. The turnaround time for this project was in the insanely speedy category—two days total. I'm glad I was able to hit on a good solution that was really well received.

LINZIE HUNTER

LONDON

WWW.LINZIEHUNTER.CO.UK

LINZIE HUNTER IS A SCOTTISH-BORN FREELANCE ILLUSTRATOR AND LETTERING ARTIST BASED IN LONDON. HER INTERNATIONAL CLIENTS INCLUDE *TIME* MAGAZINE, *THE GUARDIAN*, *THE WASHINGTON POST*, *THE WALL STREET JOURNAL*, HALLMARK, NIKE, VH1, GILLETTE, SKINNY COW, THE BBC, RANDOM HOUSE, PENGUIN, AND CHRONICLE BOOKS. HER LETTERING WORK IS CREATED BOTH DIGITALLY AND TRADITIONALLY BY HAND. WHEN AWAY FROM THE COMPUTER, SHE ALSO ENJOYS PRINTMAKING AND SWING DANCING.

RIGHT:
WORDS USED TO
DESCRIBE PAIN

GLOBE MAGAZINE, "2012 WEEKEND FUN GUIDE" COVER

I had a tight deadline for this cover, so I created the preliminary sketch digitally rather than on paper. I like working with pen and ink, but when time does not allow, working directly in Photoshop offers some advantages. I was able to play with various color schemes for the design and create

a sketch fairly quickly. I marked out the wording very roughly at first (I had a list of phrases to include) and focused more on getting the overall look and feel of the cover before getting client approval. Then I tidied up (or in some cases, completely redrew) all the lettering and illustration, and added extra textures in Photoshop.

RIGHT:
GLOBE MAGAZINE,
"2012 WEEKEND
FUN GUIDE" COVER

TOBIAS HALL

LONDON

WWW.TOBIAS-HALL.CO.UK

TOBIAS HALL IS A FREELANCE ILLUSTRATOR, LETTERER, DESIGNER, AND MURAL ARTIST IN LONDON. SINCE GRADUATING FROM DESIGN SCHOOL IN 2010, HE'S BEEN WORKING CLOSELY WITH THE UK-BASED ITALIAN RESTAURANT CHAIN ZIZZI AS THEIR IN-HOUSE ILLUSTRATOR, DESIGNER, AND ART DIRECTOR. HE'S ALSO BEEN LUCKY ENOUGH TO WORK ON AN ECLECTIC MIX OF PROJECTS FOR A GROWING LIST OF INTERNATIONAL CLIENTS. HALL LIKES TO DRAW STUFF INSPIRED BY THE MUSIC THAT HE LISTENS TO OR THE THINGS THAT HE READS.

RIGHT:
ZIZZI CHILLI OIL
AND OLIVE OIL

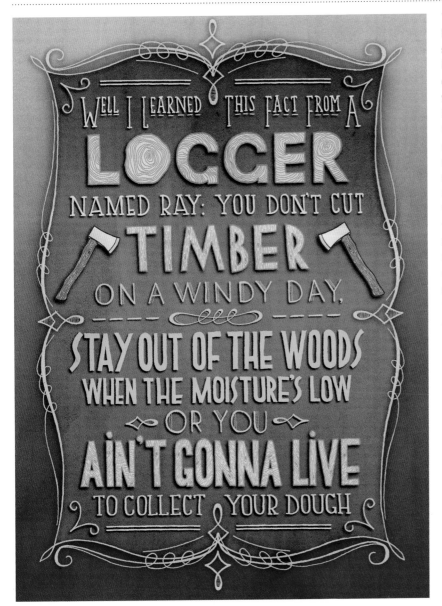

THE LUMBERJACK, *AMMO MAGAZINE*

I started this project by doing a quick sketch to get an idea of proportions and how I was going to achieve emphasis on certain words and lines. For instance, the words "logger," "timber," and "ain't gonna live" needed the most prominence within the composition. Then, I started drawing each line on various bits of A3 before scanning them into Photoshop, correcting any issues with spacing, etc., and adding rough color. The ornaments and border in this piece were inspired, in part, by those on the Jack Daniel's bottle labels. These were sketched out separately. Often, I'll print out the text layout by itself at a very low opacity so I know exactly where the border and ornaments need to go to best frame the lettering. Finally, I'll add shadow, texture, and tone to the piece.

MARY KATE MCDEVITT

BROOKLYN, NEW YORK

WWW.MARYKATEMCDEVITT.COM

MARY KATE MCDEVITT IS A LETTERER AND ILLUSTRATOR BASED IN BROOKLYN. MCDEVITT GREW UP IN PENNSYLVANIA AND WENT TO THE TYLER SCHOOL OF ART TO STUDY DESIGN AND ILLUSTRATION. AFTER WORKING AT A DESIGN STUDIO FOR TWO YEARS AFTER GRADUATION, SHE FOUND HER REAL PASSION FOR LETTERING AFTER OPENING AN ETSY SHOP AND SELLING HANDMADE AND HAND-LETTERED GOODS. MCDEVITT WORKS WITH A VARIETY OF CLIENTS FOR JUST ABOUT ANYTHING THAT CALLS FOR LETTERING.

PLEASE TELL US ABOUT YOUR ART AND DESIGN BACKGROUND.

I went to Tyler School of Art and took painting, sculpture, fabric, and drawing classes but ultimately ended up in design because I loved the assignments and the problem solving that went along with branding and packaging design. Because I love drawing and illustration, my design projects ended up having a lot of hand-drawn elements, textures, and illustration, which led to my love of hand-drawn lettering.

TELL US ABOUT WHY YOU LOVE NOSTALGIA AND THINGS FROM THE PAST?

I was just looking at a photo of New York from the 1930s, and while that time in America was very tough, it's hard not to look at the beauty of all the signage, the men in suits, and the overall attention to detail in design and architecture that we just don't have today. Everything was done by hand. The invention of the vinyl-sign printer pretty much ruined the way our cities look.

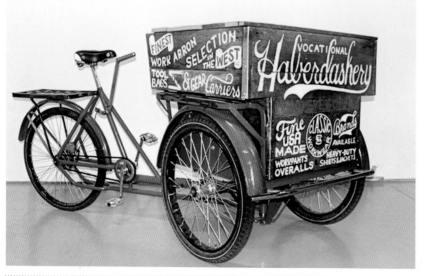

LEFT:
HAND-EYE
SUPPLY TRIKE

YOUR WORK HAS A LOVELY WARMTH AND HOMEYNESS TO IT. IS THAT SOMETHING YOU WORK HARD TO ACHIEVE?

My work is pretty casual. While I do love detail-oriented pieces, everything I do is hand drawn with very little fussiness. I love using historical references for my work, and I take that inspiration and interpret it in my own style. I think giving your work your own personal style gives it that warmth—it's the next best thing to meeting the artist in person.

IS THERE ANY SPECIAL MATERIAL OR MEDIUM YOU WOULD LOVE TO EXPERIMENT WITH FOR YOUR NEXT PROJECT?

I used to do a lot more painting for my illustration; that is something I would like to get back into. I work with hand-painted textures and all my lettering is done by hand, but the final look is made on the computer. Time is really the only issue; it's difficult to work like that (for me—I know there are still illustrators working in oil paint) for client projects when deadlines are in and out of my planner. That's why I like to work on a lot of personal projects, to experiment with different media. I will not be tempted to get a Cintiq; I just can't imagine ditching my beloved paper for a screen and a fake pen. But the time-saving aspect is appealing.

LEFT:
HAND-EYE
SUPPLY
BANDANA

ABOVE:
HUNKER DOWN

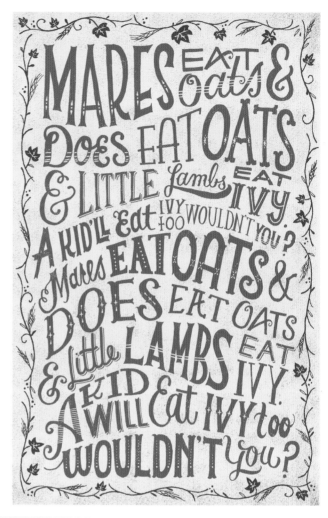

BELOW:
LET'S BRING BACK,
P'S AND Q'S

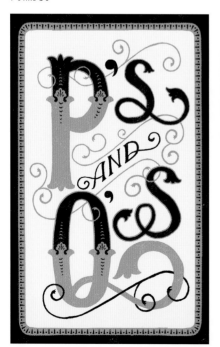

BELOW:
HP BANNER SECOND
LOCATION

COFFEE LOVERS

I was asked to show my work at one of my favorite coffee shops in Portland, Oregon, called Ristretto Roasters. I came up with the idea of doing a collection of postcards inspired by vintage coffee labels. I initially wanted a large poster of the collection of cards and perforate them so you could take it apart, but the holes looked too small in comparison to the poster, so that idea was nixed. However, I felt the look came across in the end anyway so it worked out. I came up with as many coffee-related phrases as possible and started sketching out 4 X 6-inch (10 X 15 cm) designs. Once I got my favorites, I inked them up, scanned them in, and arranged them on the computer. My printer (who is also my boyfriend), Man Vs Ink, printed them on Rives BFK, and the limited edition came out beautifully.

CHRIS PIASCIK
HARTFORD, CONNECTICUT
WWW.CHRISPIASCIK.COM

CHRIS PIASCIK IS AN INDEPENDENT ILLUSTRATOR AND DESIGNER RESIDING IN CONNECTICUT. SINCE GRADUATING FROM THE HARTFORD ART SCHOOL WITH DEGREES IN VISUAL COMMUNICATION DESIGN AND ART HISTORY, HE HAS WORKED AT TWO AWARD-WINNING DESIGN FIRMS WHILE ACTIVELY PURSUING HIS PERSONAL WORK AND EXHIBITING IT IN MANY SOLO AND GROUP SHOWS. PIASCIK HAS BEEN POSTING A NEW DRAWING ON HIS BLOG EVERY WEEKDAY SINCE LATE 2007. EARLY IN 2012, HE SELF-PUBLISHED A BOOK FEATURING THE FIRST 1,000 DRAWINGS, WHICH WENT ON TO WIN SEVERAL DESIGN AWARDS.

RIGHT:
ALL MY
BIKES BOOK

MORGAN & MILO SHOEBOX

I worked with the design studio Moth to create the Morgan & Milo shoeboxes. The boxes are designed to promote recycling and encourage the end user to keep the box. They are covered with puzzles, games, mazes, riddles, quotes, and fun characters. They are craft boxes screen-printed with white and green. While creating the illustrations, I broke the box down into separate panels and began drawing and refining to fit in as many games and fun quotes as I could. The lettering was done as loose and playful as possible to be very approachable and fun for the children who would be interacting with the boxes.

DINARA MIRTALIPOVA

TWINSBURG, OHIO

WWW.MIRDINARA.COM

DINARA MIRTALIPOVA IS AN UZBEK ARTIST AND CHILDREN'S BOOK ILLUSTRATOR. SHE IS KNOWN FOR BOLD, FOLKSY FLORAL PATTERNS, AS WELL AS FOR ARTWORK INSPIRED BY MYTH AND WONDER. MIRTALIPOVA GRADUATED FROM THE UNIVERSITY OF ECONOMICS IN TASHKENT, UZBEKISTAN, WITH A MAJOR IN CYBERNETICS. SHE DISCOVERED HER PASSION FOR DRAWING SHORTLY AFTER FINISHING SCHOOL AND DECIDED TO PURSUE A MORE ARTISTIC CAREER. FINDING INSPIRATION IN FOLK MUSIC AND FAIRY TALES, MIRTALIPOVA IS A DREAMER WHO CAPTURES FANTASY IN HER ILLUSTRATIONS.

LEFT:
LOVE & BE LOVED

ENJOY

Drawing, for me, is like reading a book. I don't like sketching because it's like peeking at the end of the book and finding out the plot. I prefer to start with a blank page and just draw lines. As I'm drawing, I'm figuring out what it is that I'm drawing. This piece, for example, started with the letter *n* and the flower above it. And my hand just wanted to bring down the stroke for the *j* and that's how the word "enjoy" appeared.

BELOW:
ENJOY

ASHLEY HOHNSTEIN

MINNEAPOLIS

WWW.ASHLEYHOHNSTEIN.COM

ASHLEY HOHNSTEIN IS A GRAPHIC DESIGNER WHO ENJOYS EXPLORING HAND LETTERING AND ILLUSTRATION AND THEIR APPLICATIONS IN GRAPHIC DESIGN. THROUGH BOLD COLORS, STRONG TYPE, AND COMPELLING CONCEPTS, SHE CREATES BEAUTIFUL WORK. WHEN SHE ISN'T DOODLING LETTERFORMS OR THINKING AHEAD TO HER NEXT PROJECT, SHE IS IMMERSED IN SOME ARTICLE ON THE INTERNET ABOUT CULTURE OR MUSIC, DAYDREAMING ABOUT THE DOGS SHE'LL OWN SOMEDAY, OR ON THE HUNT FOR VINTAGE TYPE EPHEMERA TO COVER THE WALLS OF HER APARTMENT.

RIGHT:
GOOD LIFE MUESLI DETAIL

GOOD LIFE MÜESLI DETAIL

When I approached this project, I knew I wanted to emphasize the raw ingredients of the müesli through the illustrations and type. I started with some rough doodles in pencil and began layering up refinements on tracing paper (typically redrawn in felt tip markers at varying widths). Once I was happy with the refinement, I scanned it into my computer. Then I cleaned up the edges, made adjustments in Photoshop, and ended with a conversion into a bitmap file. These bitmap files were placed into my layout in Illustrator. I then messed around with the placement and size until I was happy with the results! Bitmap files are perfect for this sort of piece because they can change colors in Illustrator and maintain a hand-lettered feel.

LEFT:
GOOD LIFE MÜESLI DETAIL

ABCDE
FGHIJK
LMNOP
QRSTU
VWXYZ

ABOVE:
FOOFARAW
TYPEFACE

LEFT:
JERK SODA
PACKAGING

FRANCESCO POROLI

MILAN

WWW.FRANCESCOPOROLI.IT

FRANCESCO POROLI IS A FREELANCE ART DIRECTOR AND ILLUSTRATOR BASED IN MILAN. SINCE 2000, HE HAS WORKED FOR A WIDE RANGE OF CLIENTS, INCLUDING *THE NEW YORK TIMES MAGAZINE*, *WIRED*, GOOGLE, THE NBA, ADIDAS, AND MORE.

RIGHT:
RIVISTA UFFICIALE NBA MAGAZINE COVERS

RIVISTA UFFICIALE NBA
MAGAZINE COVERS

Rivista Ufficiale NBA is the official—and only—NBA magazine in Italy. Editorial content and graphic design are done by the in-house editorial staff. I printed out the cover with the chosen photo and the bold logo and then started to draw all the text around these elements, trying to fill all the space. Then everything was scanned and imported into Photoshop. For the New York issue, I just inverted the color from black to white, because I wanted to have a real rough, handwritten feeling on the cover. In the interview issue, I played around with the team colors, which stood out nicely against the white background and player's uniform.

C86, MATT LYON
LONDON
WWW.C8SIX.COM

MATT LYON IS A GRAPHIC ARTIST AND ILLUSTRATOR WHOSE WORK EXPLORES RECURRING MOTIFS AND THEMES THAT INCLUDE AN INTEREST IN FANTASTICAL BUILDINGS, MACHINES, AND ABSTRACTIONS. IN ADDITION, HE WORKS EXTENSIVELY WITH DRAWING AND TYPOGRAPHY, CONTINUING HIS PERSONAL STYLE WITH DESIGNS THAT ARE SOMETIMES GEOMETRIC OR WHIMSICAL, OFTEN VIBRANTLY COLORED, AND ALWAYS LIVELY. HE HAS WORKED FOR AOL, AT&T, MICROSOFT, AND OTHER GLOBAL CLIENTS, AND HIS DESIGNS HAVE BEEN WIDELY SEEN IN BOOKS, MAGAZINES, AND EXHIBITIONS WORLDWIDE.

LEFT:
I AM THE
DREAMER

RIGHT:
MAMA TOLD YOU
NOT TO LOOT

IMAGINARY PARADISE

This design was inspired by a quote by Simone Weil: "We must prefer real hell to an imaginary paradise." All of my work starts as a black ink drawing on paper. I use a fountain pen or brush pen rather than a pencil because it forces immediacy in committing a line to paper, rather than sketching and erasing mistakes. As such, I find that I concentrate more while embracing anything unexpected during the process. Once complete, the line work is redrawn in Adobe Illustrator using the pen tool before applying a provisionary palette of colors. Working in Photoshop, I apply final color adjustments, composition layouts, and texturing to finish the design.

LEFT:
IMAGINARY
PARADISE

STEVE SIMPSON
DUBLIN
WWW.STEVESIMPSON.COM

WITH MORE THAN THIRTY YEARS' EXPERIENCE, STEVE SIMPSON TAKES A WHIMSICAL APPROACH TO HIS WORK THAT HAS EARNED HIM TOP INTERNATIONAL AWARDS FOR ILLUSTRATION, PACKAGING DESIGN, AND CHILDREN'S BOOK ART. SIMPSON'S WORK HAS BEEN EXHIBITED IN LONDON, LOS ANGELES, AND NEW YORK AND HAS BEEN FEATURED IN MANY PROMINENT MAGAZINES AND BLOGS GLOBALLY. HE IS ORIGINALLY FROM THE UK BUT HAS MADE IRELAND HIS HOME FOR THE PAST TWENTY YEARS.

HOW THE WHALE GOT HIS THROAT

I tend to have pet projects—things that hang around my sketchbooks until I've built up enough steam working on client projects that, even if I'm crazy busy, I just have to complete. They usually start with an idea, a quick thumbnail, quite often sparked by another unrelated project. They may well stay a thumbnail for several months. Once I decide to tackle the project, it's quite fast. I'll do as many sketches as it takes to exhaust as many options as needed for me to believe my initial idea was the best way to go. I then scan it into Photoshop and work it up. For something like this, there's probably about ten hours work in it. The sense of achievement and contentment I get from these personal projects gives me renewed energy for the occasionally less exciting paying projects.

LEFT:
HOW THE WHALE
GOT HIS THROAT

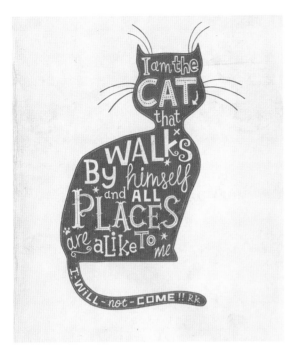

ALEJANDRO GIRALDO
MEDELLÍN, COLOMBIA
WWW.ALEJOGIRALDO.COM

ALEJANDRO GIRALDO IS A GRAPHIC DESIGNER, ILLUSTRATOR, AND ART DIRECTOR FROM MEDELLÍN, COLOMBIA. HE HOLDS A MASTER OF ARTS DEGREE IN ART DIRECTION FROM THE BARCELONA SCHOOL OF DESIGN. CURRENTLY, HE SPENDS HIS TIME WORKING ON FREELANCE PROJECTS RELATED TO ILLUSTRATION AND FASHION AS WELL AS TEACHING GRAPHIC DESIGN AND ILLUSTRATION AT THE UNIVERSITY LEVEL. HIS WORK HAS BEEN FEATURED IN NUMEROUS PUBLICATIONS AND HAS BEEN ON DISPLAY IN SHOWS IN MEDELLÍN AND SEOUL, SOUTH KOREA.

FAR LEFT:
YOU BE THE
ANCHOR

LEFT:
AMIGOS LATIN
LOVER

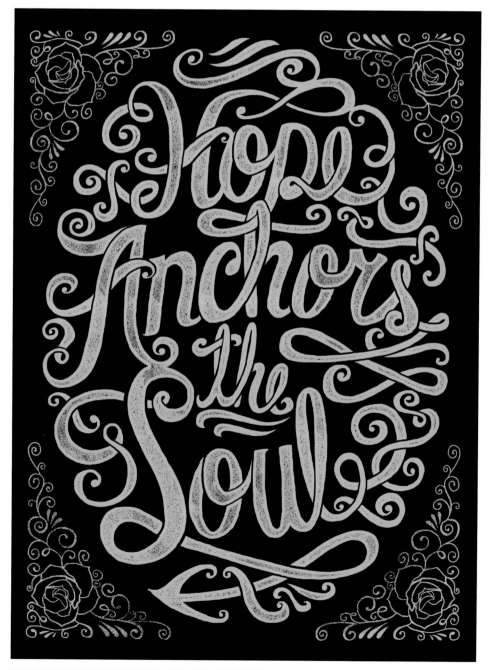

HOPE

I think inspiration is key in my creative process. I always find it in songs, movies, or just in a simple conversation. I start by thinking and shaping an idea in my mind. After that, I make a rough sketch in my notebook and then scan it into Photoshop. Sometimes, I love to be experimental and output my drawings as a wood engraving or silkscreen print.

TIMBA SMITS
LONDON
WWW.TIMBASMITS.COM

TIMBA SMITS IS A DESIGNER,
ARTIST, ILLUSTRATOR,
HIGH ACHIEVER, MENTOR,
PHILANTHROPIST, AND CRIME
FIGHTER (TRUE STORY). ALWAYS
THINKING, ALWAYS CREATIVE,
SMITS DOESN'T STOP VERY
OFTEN—UNLESS IT'S TO SIT AND
WATCH A GOOD FILM, BREATHE
DEEPLY, OR WATCH CLOUDS
FLOAT BY.

RIGHT:
DEPHECT T-SHIRT
EVERLASTING INK

WHAT IS YOUR ART AND DESIGN BACKGROUND, AND WHAT MADE YOU BECOME INTERESTED IN TYPOGRAPHY?

I got into art at a very early age. I'll always remember winning the grade 6 drawing competition for my super-rad drawing of Raphael (my favorite Teenage Mutant Ninja Turtle) as the kick start that led me on my journey into art and design. I never studied, I just did it, and the more I worked at it, the better I became. I started off in fine art, painting, and I even opened a number of successful art galleries with some friends while living in Melbourne, Australia.

It wasn't until I decided to start my own lowbrow art magazine with a mate (*Wooden Toy Quarterly*, 2006–2011), that I really got into design and type in a big way. I found that my art and illustration ability complemented my new graphic design aesthetic really well, and fusing these together in an editorial direction proved to be quite a refreshing challenge for me at the time. Type became a major part of the work I was doing on the magazine, and a real interest began to grow both within and outside of the magazine, which has led me to where I am today— obsessed by a good piece of type.

HOW DID YOU COME UP WITH YOUR STYLE?

To tell you the truth, I've never quite known how to describe my style, so I'm going to be naughty and skip over this point, leaving others to decide what my style is to them. However, I can tell you that my style comes from combining everything that I love as reference into a mixing bowl, making it quite original and a reflection of my own personal tastes. This can be anything and everything from cult 1980s movies to 1960s advertising characters and candy packaging from when I was a kid.

LEFT:
JOHNNY CUPCAKES
T-SHIRT, HOW DESIGN
LIVE 2013

The main characteristic in my work is the bold fusion of illustration, faded colors, and lots—and I mean *lots*—of type. I'm a real sucker for little details, so there's always a lot going on in my work to create a unique narrative and a way to fill up space. I definitely fell asleep during "Less Is More 101," and even skipped a number of "Keep It Simple" classes, too. I love cramming as much as possible into a piece, without overdoing it. That is the challenge.

DO YOU THINK IT'S IMPORTANT TO GET BACK TO BASICS WITH TYPOGRAPHY AND DESIGN IN GENERAL, NOT ONLY TO UNDERSTAND THE FUNDAMENTALS BUT TO ALSO REINVENT AND STAY INSPIRED? Definitely. I think that with any form of creativity, whether it be design, illustration, or type, it should be personal. Sure, it can be important at times to know the fundamentals, the history of design and type, and all its ins-and-outs, but, more often than not, it's the kid locked away in his studio, away from it all, breaking convention and throwing out all the rules who has the best chance to reinvent the wheel. I believe originality comes from looking within and deciding what is it about me that I can use throughout my art to create an influential style for others to be inspired by.

RIGHT:
KEEP CUP SALUTE
THE REUSER

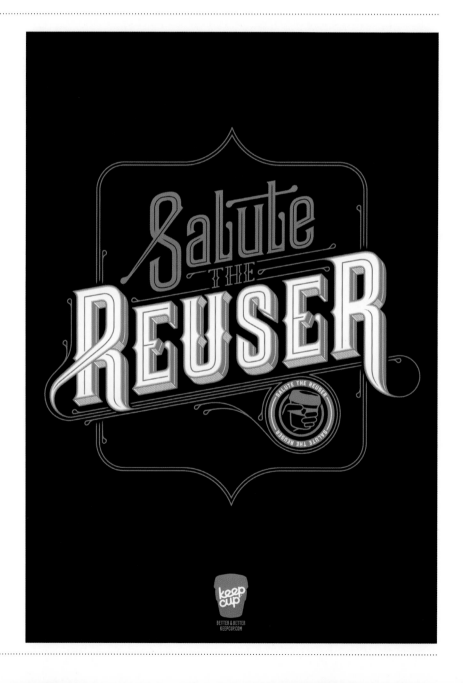

45 **R.P.M**

-ANOTHER- **7**
SECRET 7
OFFICIAL
Recording

B-SIDE

- PRODUCED IN -

STEREO

ILLUSTRATIVE TYPOGRAPHY CAN BE BOTH CONCEIVED BY HAND AND WITH A COMPUTER. THE AESTHETICS OF THESE TWO PROCESSES WILL ALWAYS DIFFER, WHICH DO YOU PREFER AND WHY?

I will always hold a candle for a more traditional approach to illustration and type—create work by hand—but I also really love the possibilities of what you can do on a computer. It also depends on the project—personal versus commercial and who or what it's for.

I prefer to jump between the two to create an interesting marriage of analog and digital resulting in my own personal style. Rarely will I start and finish a project solely using the computer. There is always a heavy amount of scanning and jumping back and forth between my drawing table and my computer station, and I love this process. After all, who really enjoys staring at a screen all day long? At the end of the day, for me, pencil beats mouse. I call it "getting back to nature."

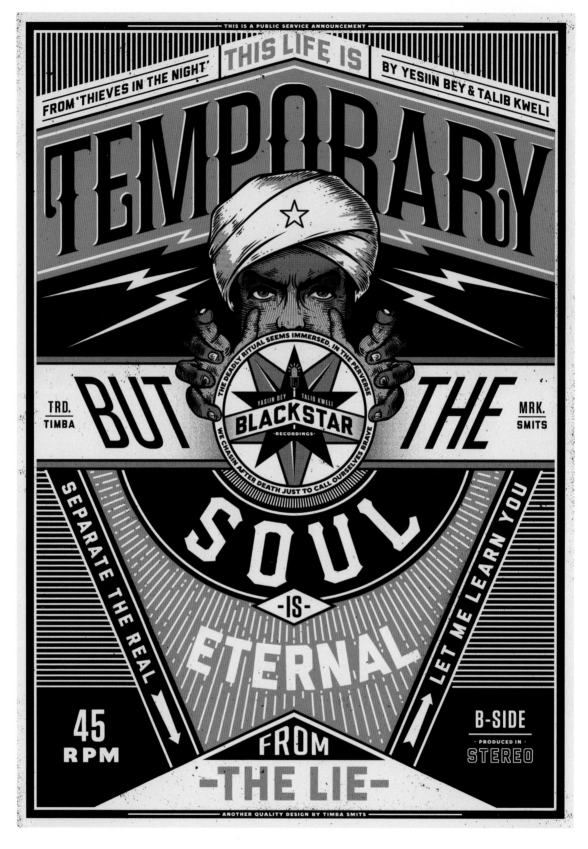

THIS PAGE:
TIMBA SMITS'S
HANDMADE TYPEFACE

WHAT WAS THE PROCESS YOU FOLLOWED TO CREATE YOUR HANDMADE TYPEFACE?

At first, my intention was to create a typographic illustration for the outside packaging of *Wooden Toy Quarterly*, 6. The theme of the issue was "handmade," so the piece had to reflect the nature of creating art and design by hand. I went ahead and drew the letters using pencils and gouache. After

I finished the desired type for the packaging, I couldn't help but continue, completing a full alphabet to use throughout the issue. I call it Sticks & Twine.

It was a very natural, albeit time-consuming, process to create the typeface beginning with my outlines and then going over them with gouache colors and building up to all the details and shading using various grades of HB to 4B pencils.

SAMUEL JACQUES

MONTREAL

WWW.SJACQUES.COM

SAMUEL JACQUES IS AN ILLUSTRATOR, ANIMATOR, AND TYPE DESIGNER BASED IN MONTREAL. HIS WORK HAS BEEN FEATURED IN *COMMUNICATION ARTS*, *TYPE DIRECTORS CLUB ANNUAL*, *PRIX GRAFIKA*, AND *APPLIED ARTS*.

LE NTE POSTER SERIES

It's not every day that a client comes to you and says they want hand-drawn typography for their branding and nothing more. Because this is a series of plays for a theater, it's a perfect match to embrace the heritage of old typographic theater posters. With that constraint in mind, I drew different kinds of type that you wouldn't usually see together. Each poster's type was in correlation with the play.

OPPOSITE/BELOW:
LE NTE POSTER SERIES

DESIGN REFORM COUNCIL, JACKKRIT ANANTAKUL

BANGKOK

WWW.DESIGNREFORMCOUNCIL.COM

DESIGN REFORM COUNCIL WAS ESTABLISHED IN 2006 BY JACKKRIT ANANTAKUL. HE IS A GRAPHIC DESIGNER, ILLUSTRATOR, AND TYPE DESIGNER.

BELOW: RIGHT:
EVIL   THAI FIGHT
          FLOOD

CAROLYN SEWELL
WASHINGTON, D.C.
WWW.CAROLYNSEWELL.COM

CAROLYN IS A SERIOUS DOODLER IN LOVE WITH ALL THINGS UNICORNY AND TYPOGRAPHIC. IT WAS DURING EIGHTH GRADE STUDY HALL THAT SHE KNEW SHE WANTED TO BE A GRAPHIC DESIGNER. WHILE OTHER STUDENTS WERE DOING HOMEWORK, SHE WAS HAND-LETTERING HER FRIENDS' BOOK COVERS FOR $1 ($2 IF YOU WANTED PAISLEY). BOOK COVERS BECAME PEP RALLY SIGNS, AND COLLEGE PROJECTS BECAME PAYING CLIENTS. HER WORK HAS BEEN PUBLISHED IN *COMMUNICATION ARTS*, *GRAFIK*, *HOW*, *GDUSA*, *CMYK* MAGAZINE, AND *UPPERCASE*. CAROLYN RECENTLY EXHIBITED A YEARLONG PROJECT OF DAILY HAND-DRAWN "POSTCARDS TO MY PARENTS" AND IS CURRENTLY WORKING ON THE FOLLOW-UP PROJECT, "POSTCARDS TO MY PEEPS."

ABOVE:
WEDDING POSTER FOR
ANNA & DANIEL

AIGA DC NOTECARD

Washington, DC's local AIGA chapter needed a general notecard that could work for all its correspondence (welcoming new members, thanking sponsors), so the wording couldn't be too specific. We agreed to use only the club name, and I took pencil to paper and started sketching. I soon realized I was drawing each word to fit around the next, and before long I had a big sheet of AIGADCs. Once the composition was set, I traced everything with pen, scanned and cleaned it in Photoshop, vectorized and colored the words in Illustrator, and then brought it back into Photoshop to add texture.

ABOVE:
AIGA DC
NOTECARD

WASTE STUDIO, NORMAN HAYES
NOTTINGHAM, ENGLAND
WASTESTUDIO.COM

NORMAN HAYES IS THE CREATIVE DIRECTOR AND COFOUNDER OF WASTE STUDIO, AN AWARD-WINNING, INDEPENDENT CREATIVE AGENCY. WASTE STUDIO IS A COLLABORATIVE, DIVERSE, AND FORWARD-THINKING TEAM THAT HAS A GENUINE PASSION FOR WHAT THEY DO. WASTE DELIVERS CONSIDERED AND ENGAGING DESIGN FOR A WIDE RANGE OF CLIENTS ACROSS BOTH THE PRIVATE AND PUBLIC SECTORS.

WOODEN TOY QUARTERLY
MAGAZINE PACKAGING

WHAT IS YOUR ART AND DESIGN BACKGROUND?

My love for typography came about while studying graphic design in college, when I was introduced to the wonderful work of Neville Brody and David Carson. It was a turning point for me, as I had always looked at type as information. But after seeing *Emigre* and *Ray Gun* magazines, I realized type can be used as image, and legibility wasn't always important. From this point on, I began experimenting with type and working with it as image.

HOW DID YOU DEVELOP YOUR STYLE?

Not entirely sure, really. I did work from a very early age at a theme park and zoo called Flamingoland in the North Yorkshire Moors, and spent the lengthy summers living in a caravan there and being surrounded by elaborate fairground rides, badly made character costumes, and a pretty awesome zoo. That had to have made some impression on me.

I would say we really started to take our style seriously when we were approached by creative publications and blogs asking if they could do a feature on Waste. We became known for our odd characters that we would combine with our hand-drawn letterforms.

YOUR WORK AND DESIGN PHILOSOPHY HAS A DISTINCT HANDS-ON QUALITY TO IT. HAVE YOU ALWAYS WORKED THIS WAY?

Our work is massively influenced by old printing traditions such as silkscreen printing and letterpress printing, and we love to get away from the computer and get our hands dirty. I guess it is this that gives our work a hands-on quality.

DO YOU THINK DRAWING TYPE AND LETTERS BY HAND IS AN IMPORTANT THING TO PRACTICE?

I think the only way to truly understand letterforms is to simply spend time drawing them. It's during this process that you begin to really understand the construction of the letter.

WASTE & GRINGO RECORDS presents BANDIT

AN EVENING OF LIVE MUSIC AND SCREEN PRINTING

THAT FUCKING TANK

New Album Release TANKNOLOGY

STAGEBLOOD.

Members of Lords Mogwai and Eska

OX SCAPULA

AWKWARD Rolls RHYTHMS AND KLANGS FROM STOKE!

PETER PARKER AS PARKERTRON FINGATHING

28th MARCH DOORS 7PM £4/3

AT THE ART ORG 21 STATION ST

FEATURING WORK BY ~
~ JOCOPE / WASTE / OILK /
/DAVID FORD/ SPINSTERS EMPORIUM PR
/ JENNIE WEBBER / CALVIN SANGSTER / BA

MORE INFO: WWW.WASTEYOURSE

SUPPORTED BY: LONESS

FLOODIT POSTERS

I pretty much have a little A to Z
route I tend to take for these projects.
Normally my ideas take on life in
sketchbooks and then are scanned
and printed as a base to build on. This
happens until I'm happy with the
composition. Then, I scan and print out
a final version in 10 percent opacity so
I can barely see the design. I then use
brush and ink to create my final line
art layer. Most of the time, I'll scan
the finished art and color it up on the
computer, both to simplify the process
and to allow me to play around with color
combinations, etc. Since most of my
work is silkscreened, I find this little
route works every time.

MWM GRAPHICS, MATT W. MOORE

PORTLAND, MAINE

WWW.MWMGRAPHICS.COM

MATT W. MOORE HAS DUBBED HIS DIGITAL ABSTRACT STYLE "VECTORFUNK" AND HAS EMPLOYED IT TO COVER SURFACES RANGING FROM RAY-BAN WAYFARERS TO ALMOND SURFBOARDS TO COCA-COLA'S LONDON OLYMPICS CAMPAIGN. WHETHER WORKING IN FINE ART OR COMMERCIAL APPLICATIONS, MOORE FINDS THAT EACH SPARKS THE OTHER. GRAPHIC DESIGN PROJECTS OFTEN INFORM THE "MONUMENTAL MURALS" HE PAINTS IN NEIGHBORHOODS AROUND THE WORLD. HIS ANNUAL SERIES OF WATERCOLOR PAINTINGS IN BLACK AND WHITE MIGHT INFORM FUTURE LOGO DESIGNS. CROSS-POLLINATING BETWEEN DISCIPLINES ALLOWS HIM TO REFRESH HIS PERSPECTIVE AND PRODUCE UNIQUE WORK.

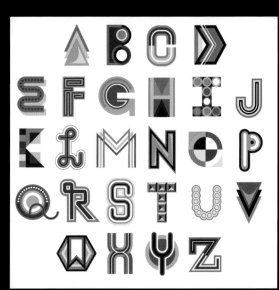

FAR LEFT:
ALPHAFONT 1

LEFT:
ALPHAFONT 2

VAULT49
NEW YORK CITY
WWW.VAULT49.COM

VAULT49 IS A BOUTIQUE DESIGN STUDIO, ARTISTIC COLLABORATION, AND PLAYGROUND FOUNDED IN 2002 BY JONATHAN KENYON AND JOHN GLASGOW. THE STUDIO PRODUCES WORK CHARACTERIZED BY A FOCUS ON CRAFTSMANSHIP, MULTIMEDIA, AND AN EXPRESSIVE USE OF COLOR. IN A CREATIVE WORLD THAT IS INCREASINGLY DIGITAL, VAULT49'S BROAD PORTFOLIO COMBINES TECHNOLOGY WITH ALL-IMPORTANT CRAFTSMANSHIP AND NATURAL ABILITY, GIVING IT AN AUTHENTICITY THAT IS IMPOSSIBLE TO REPLICATE.

LEFT:
HAND-PAINTED
SAWS

SCREEN-PRINTED TABLE

When working on the table design for the Vault49 studio, we wanted to ensure we represented the amazing city of New York that we are all fortunate enough to be a part of. So we sourced the wood from upstate, drove it back to the city, carried it up five floors to the studio, and built the table from scratch. We then started on the customization process.

We set about listing all the areas that were important to the studio and the people who work here to ensure it had a lot of nice hidden meaning and messaging. Once the list was organized, we quickly designed the artwork using custom and standard typefaces combined with a bit of illustration. This was then output as films on our in-house large-format printer.

We then exposed the artwork onto giant screens at our downtown screen-print studio and printed the design directly onto the tabletop. Once dry, we sanded the printing to give it a distressed look and coated the whole table with four coats of varnish and a layer of wax to give the final article a really fantastic end result.

THIS PAGE:
SCREEN-PRINTED
TABLE

CHAPTER 4

CONTEMPORARY
TYPE

THE DEFINITION OF CONTEMPORARY IS "FOLLOWING MODERN
IDEAS IN STYLE OR DESIGN." THE DESIGNERS IN THIS
CHAPTER USE THE MOST UP-TO-DATE TECHNIQUES AND
TECHNOLOGY TO CREATE THEIR MODERN TYPE DESIGNS.

GIULIA SANTOPADRE
ROME
WWW.GIULIASANTOPADRE.COM

GIULIA SANTOPADRE IS AN ILLUSTRATOR, GRAPHIC DESIGNER, AND TYPE DESIGNER IN ROME. SHE GRADUATED FROM THE ISTITUTO EUROPEO DI DESIGN IN ROME IN 2006 WITH A DEGREE IN GRAPHIC DESIGN.

GROW YOUR OWN DESIGNER

A few years back, at the beginning of my design career, I had been looking for a way to promote myself. I came up with the idea of growth, of being an investment to the company that would hire me. Also, I wanted to immediately show off what I considered to be my best skill: typography. So this became my portfolio cover. As most illustrators and designers do, I always start off sketching on paper and then scan and sometimes trace. I start adding details and fine-tuning, and then I have to stop myself before I get obsessive; that's the part I find the most difficult.

ABOVE:
FRULLATO

BEN JOHNSTON

TORONTO

WWW.BEHANCE.NET/BENJOHNSTON

CANADIAN-BORN BEN JOHNSTON IS A SELF-TAUGHT DESIGNER WHO GREW UP IN CAPE TOWN, SOUTH AFRICA. AFTER A BRIEF STINT IN INDUSTRIAL DESIGN, JOHNSTON STARTED FOCUSING ON TRADITIONAL GRAPHIC DESIGN, WITH A PREFERENCE FOR CREATING TYPOGRAPHIC ILLUSTRATIONS FROM SCRATCH. HIS INDUSTRIAL DESIGN EXPERIENCE GIVES HIM THE ABILITY TO BREAK THE CONFINES OF 2-D AND 3-D, ENABLING HIM TO BRING HIS DESIGNS TO LIFE. HIS PORTFOLIO INCLUDES A PROLIFIC SELECTION OF COMPLETED PROJECTS FOR RENOWNED AD AGENCIES, SOUTH AFRICAN BUSINESSES, AND MAJOR OVERSEAS CLIENTS.

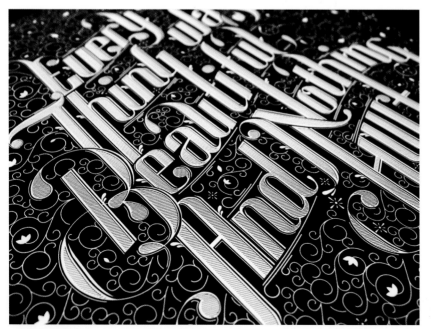

EVERYTHING WAS BEAUTIFUL AND NOTHING HURT

I always start projects by doing a few rough sketches on some scraps of paper, and once I finally figure out what I'm going to do—sometimes hours or days later—I'll do a final sketch to size. I then scan it in and start playing with the line work. With the pen tool I create a rough background around the letters, and once all the letters are the way I want them, I most likely redo the whole background and the style of it. That is one of the things I love most: that the lettering pieces constantly evolve as you do them. The end result is rarely ever the same as the initial concept sketch.

ABOVE LEFT:
THIS WAS NEVER
GOING TO BE SIMPLE

ABOVE RIGHT:
EXCUSE ME WHILE I
KISS THE SKY

FAR LEFT:
HOLEY MOLEY, MY OH
MY, YOU'RE THE APPLE
OF MY EYE

LEFT:
MAY THE BRIDGES I
BURN LIGHT THE WAY

CORY SAY

DALLAS

WWW.CARGOCOLLECTIVE.COM/CORYSAY

CORY SAY IS A TYPE DESIGNER CURRENTLY WORKING AS AN ART DIRECTOR FOR TRACYLOCKE, A NATIONAL DESIGN AND MARKETING AGENCY IN DALLAS. HE IS A CONCEPT-DRIVEN DESIGNER AND ART DIRECTOR WHO LOVES ALL FACETS OF DESIGN, BUT HE'S HEAD-OVER-HEELS IN LOVE WITH HAND LETTERING AND ILLUSTRATION.

LEFT:
MATTHEW 6:33 POSTER

JUANA LAXAGUE AND VALERIA RUIZ-SCHULZE

BUENOS AIRES

WWW.BEHANCE.NET/JUANALAXAGUE
WWW.BEHANCE.NET/VALERIARUIZSCHULZE

JUANA LAXAGUE AND VALERIA RUIZ-SCHULZE ARE GRAPHIC DESIGNERS BASED IN BUENOS AIRES. THEY HAVE APPROACHED SEVERAL PROJECTS TOGETHER BY FOCUSING ON TYPOGRAPHY AND WHAT IT COMMUNICATES THROUGH ITS FORM.

HEROES PRINT COLLECTION

In general, when we start working on a project, the first thing we develop is the idea we want to communicate. Then, we usually search for references of techniques and graphic languages that are in tune with that concept. This inspires us to create our own language and build on the project concept.

RYAN FEERER
ABILENE, TEXAS
WWW.RYANFEERER.COM

RYAN FEERER IS A DESIGNER, ILLUSTRATOR, TEACHER, AND RESTAURATEUR IN ABILENE. THIS BURLY TEXAS NATIVE DESIGNS WITH A SENSE OF HUMOR, MERGING TYPOGRAPHY AND ILLUSTRATION FOR PROJECTS RANGING FROM HOMETOWN MOM-AND-POP IDENTITIES TO INTERNATIONAL CAMPAIGNS—AS HE LIKES TO SAY, "FUN THINGS FOR FUN PEOPLE." HE EARNED AN MFA IN DESIGN FROM THE SCHOOL OF VISUAL ARTS.

ABOVE:
BETTY & JUNE
BAGS AND TAGS

LEFT:
DARK WAS THE
NIGHT

ABI-HAUS

I knew what I wanted the exterior of the restaurant to look like. It needed to be inviting, informative, and simple, with some familiarity. You should be able to glance at the painted façade and have a pretty good understanding of the type of experience you will have. The type was chosen based on the brand mark I had previously created for the restaurant. Other than that, it was just stacking the type in three categorical columns, with items in each separated by horizontal bars—and a handful of friends to help paint.

BELOW LEFT:
ABI-HAUS

BELOW RIGHT:
ABILENE I CAN FLY

CHRISTOPHER VINCA

HONOLULU

WWW.BEHANCE.NET/CHRISVINCA

CHRISTOPHER VINCA IS A DESIGNER, LETTERER, AND PHOTOGRAPHER BORN AND RAISED IN HONOLULU. HE CURRENTLY FREELANCES FOR PEOPLE ALL AROUND THE WORLD AND HAS BEEN FEATURED ON MANY DESIGN SITES, SUCH AS ABDUZEEDO, DESIGNSPIRATION, FROM UP NORTH, AND ADOBE. WHEN HE IS NOT DESIGNING, HE ENJOYS HIKING, PLAYING MUSIC, AND SURFING WITH FAMILY AND FRIENDS.

LEFT:
SURF HI-3D

DREAMS BE DREAMS 3-D

When designing typography, I always start sketching in my Moleskine notebook. Once I get a rough concept, I scan my sketches into Photoshop and print out an enlarged version. Using my sharpened lead holder and kneaded eraser, I tighten up the edges on tracing paper. I go through this cycle about two or three times until my lines are nice and clean. Then I convert my sketch into a vector using Illustrator. After it looks perfect, I'm able to drag and drop it onto my designs or extrude it three dimensionally in Cinema 4D.

LEFT/ABOVE:
**DREAMS BE DREAMS
3-D AND SKETCH**

I LOVE DUST
PORTSMOUTH, ENGLAND
WWW.ILOVEDUST.COM

IN BUSINESS SINCE 2003, I LOVE DUST IS A MULTIDISCIPLINARY DESIGN BOUTIQUE SPECIALIZING IN CREATIVE SOLUTIONS FROM GRAPHIC DESIGN AND ILLUSTRATION TO TREND PREDICTION. BASED ON THE SOUTH COAST OF ENGLAND, SURROUNDED BY ROLLING BRITISH COUNTRYSIDE AND WHIPPED BY SEA AIR, THE DESIGN TEAM IS A MELTING POT OF AWESOME UK DESIGNERS AND TALENT FROM AROUND THE GLOBE. THEY COLLABORATE WITH A DIVERSE SPECTRUM OF GLOBAL BRANDS TO CREATE FRESH, INNOVATIVE DESIGN.

RIGHT:
ALPHA WALL

OPPOSITE:
TYPOGRAPHY FOR VANS

NOTHING BUT A
HEARTACHE
EVERY DAY, YEAH
NOTHING BUT A
TEARDROP
ALL OF the way...
LOVING A BAD MAN
is such a SIN, YEAH
HE'S GOT me ALL RIGHT
CAN I GET HIM?

KENDRICK KIDD

JACKSONVILLE, FLORIDA

WWW.KENDRICKKIDD.COM

KENDRICK KIDD HAS BEEN WORKING PROFESSIONALLY AS A GRAPHIC DESIGNER FOR THE LAST FIFTEEN YEARS, AND UNPROFESSIONALLY FOR EVEN LONGER. HE HAS A LOVE FOR DESIGN, ILLUSTRATION, AND LETTERING. HE CURRENTLY WORKS AS A SENIOR ART DIRECTOR AT AN AD AGENCY IN JACKSONVILLE AND ALSO RUNS A SMALL DESIGN BUSINESS ON NIGHTS AND WEEKENDS.

TELL ME ABOUT YOUR ART AND DESIGN BACKGROUND.

The first memory I have of being exposed to art was during summer day care. The owner of the day care I attended was a fine artist and structured many of our weekly activities around music, drawing, painting, and sculpture. At the time, it all seemed pretty normal, but looking back, I feel lucky to have been exposed to so much that early in life. I continued to stay interested in fine art throughout school but noticed a shift toward graphics around the sixth grade after receiving my first Rob Roskopp skate deck. The bold illustration and hand lettering of Jim Phillips hooked me years before I would even know his name. I had no idea what design was or how to achieve the things he did, but I knew that was what I wanted to do. That feeling stuck with me through high school, and when my art teacher at the time brought in a representative from a nearby college to talk about graphic design, everything clicked.

LEFT:
THE INVITATION COMPANY
SCRIPT

OPPOSITE:
DO WHAT'S RIGHT

SUCCESS IS SIMPLE DO WHAT'S Right THE Right Way AT THE Right TIME

Arnold Glasgow

WHAT ARE YOUR FAVORITE DESIGN TOOLS?
I can't live without a mechanical pencil and pen eraser. Sketching has become a large part of my design process, much more so than when I was younger. Being able to rough out ideas before I sit down at the computer has helped me be a more efficient designer. In an odd sort of way, that little mechanical pencil lets me think freely and quickly without worrying about the details of a finished rendering. The flip side of that is my need for Adobe Illustrator. As much sketching as I do these days, I'm still not very good at it. I rely heavily on Illustrator to tweak, refine, and finish most of my projects. My favorite bit about both these media, though, is bringing them together. I want to keep my lettering and graphic renderings looking and feeling organic, despite the computer.

DO YOU THINK DRAWING TYPE AND LETTERS BY HAND IS AN IMPORTANT THING TO PRACTICE?
Absolutely. Beyond keeping us rooted to our design heritage, I think the freedom that drawing by hand gives you is important to the process of creating.

ENJOY THE BEAUTIFUL STRUGGLE

This was a fun one to work on. I spent some time on the phone with the company's owner discussing the quote prior to starting the work. Before explaining his take, he had asked me what I thought "Enjoy the Beautiful Struggle" meant. It spawned a pretty lengthy (and slightly philosophical) talk that ultimately gave me a great sense of what he was looking for in the lettering piece. I remember thinking about our conversation for several days after the call. No sketching, no rendering, just rolling the quote over in the back of my mind while cutting the lawn or driving to work. When I finally sat down in front of the TV to sketch (where all my best sketching happens), I already had a clear idea of what I wanted to do. I only sketched two or three roughs before settling on one I liked. After showing the sketch to the client the next day, there were minimal tweaks, and I was off to the computer for rendering. The final lettering piece ended up very close to the sketch, which is not typical for me. But I think spending the time up front to understand where the client was coming from, and giving myself enough time to think, helped keep the vision clear from the beginning.

DANI LOUREIRO
CAPE TOWN, SOUTH AFRICA
WWW.BEHANCE.NET/DANILOUREIRO

DANI LOUREIRO IS AN AWARD-WINNING ILLUSTRATOR AND DESIGNER WORKING IN CAPE TOWN AS A CREATIVE DIRECTOR IN ADVERTISING. SHE HAS A BFA FROM SAVANNAH COLLEGE OF ART AND DESIGN AND HAS WORKED AS A DESIGNER IN NEW YORK CITY AND CALIFORNIA. THROUGH EXTENSIVE TRAVELS SHE HAS FOUND INSPIRATION IN THE VISUAL LANGUAGE OF URBAN CULTURES AND IS INFLUENCED BY THE UNCONVENTIONAL USE OF TYPOGRAPHY IN DESIGN. SHE EXHIBITS REGULARLY AND IS INVOLVED IN AN ONGOING LOVE AFFAIR WITH CUSTOM LETTERING AND INTRICATE PENCIL SKETCHES.

BACK IN 5 MINUTES

This particular piece was for the window of a five-man typography show in Cape Town, and it needed to incorporate the five circular cutouts that revealed the artwork on the hanging wall. The design was inspired by Victorian typography, and I played around with how the letters and circular shapes fit together so that the title of the show was eye catching while still being readable. As with all custom lettering pieces, I start by sketching the letters and working out the composition in pencil on paper. After getting a rough sketch together, I scan in the artwork and redraw the type in Illustrator. I don't spend too much time getting the letters and shadows perfect in pencil, as I tweak the curves and line weights digitally— the sketch is more about the overall composition and structure of the piece. Once in Illustrator, I play around refining the letterforms and balancing the artwork. I tend to draw everything with the pen tool and do not use existing shapes to build the letterforms, as I find the letters come out smoother when drawn from scratch. Because of the fine line detail of this piece, we decided to have the artwork digitally printed into white vinyl at 8 X 10-foot (2.5 X 3 m) scale. The vinyl was then applied to the inside of the glass and the circles were carefully cut out. We chose to keep the vinyl artwork in bold black and white so that the five art pieces showing through the cutouts would stand out. The circular art pieces were done in specific colors that correlated to the walls of the gallery, which were each assigned a color palette.

ad >antage
THINK BIG! MEDIA | MARKETING | ADVERTISING

BELOW:
ADVANTAGE COVER
SKETCH

RIGHT:
ADVANTAGE COVER

VELCROSUIT, ADAM HILL
CAPE TOWN, SOUTH AFRICA
WWW.VELCROSUIT.COM

ADAM HILL IS A GRAPHIC DESIGNER, ILLUSTRATOR, AND MUSICIAN WHO SPENDS HIS NIGHTS AND DAYS JUGGLING HIS TWO PASSIONS—MUSIC AND DESIGN. HE HAS WORKED WITH LARGE BRANDS AND SMALL STARTUPS, EXECUTING HIS DESIGNS IN BOTH PRINT AND DIGITAL MEDIA.

ROCK 'N INK T-SHIRT

The main typography for this project needed to work as a stand-alone element later on, so that was my first consideration when I started sketching. After finding a suitable typeface to augment and customize, I realized that a guitar pick shape would create an easily understood holding device. I then moved on to writing a few lines of playful copy to fill the negative spaces. I refined the layout and then added extra textures and dirt to match the subject.

OPPOSITE:
HOT BUTTONS

HOT BUTTONS

WH TECH GUIDE 2011

ANDRÉ BEATO

LISBON

WWW.ANDREBEATO.COM

ANDRÉ BEATO IS A PORTUGUESE GRAPHIC DESIGNER AND ILLUSTRATOR. HIS WORK IS AN AMALGAMATION OF ILLUSTRATION, TYPOGRAPHY, AND TEXTURES, PLAYING WITH DIFFERENT LANGUAGES. HE IS GREATLY INFLUENCED BY THE 1980S AND DRAWS INSPIRATION FROM MOVIES AND MUSIC. HIP-HOP AND THE GRAFFITI CULTURE ARE WHERE HE STARTED TO MODIFY LETTER CHARACTERS AND PLAY WITH TYPOGRAPHY. HE HAS BEEN WORKING IN THE VARIOUS CREATIVE FIELDS OF GRAPHIC, PRINT, AND EDITORIAL, COLLABORATING WITH CLIENTS SUCH AS MAGAZINES, CLOTHING COMPANIES, AND ADVERTISING AGENCIES.

PLAYGROUND LOVE

For this design, I first decided the best way to display and define the structure block type. I did some rough sketches just to have an idea how it would look like, and then I found the typeface that suited the design the best. In this case, I decided to play with a bold and regular condensed face (sometimes I draw a custom typeface or work, but with this one I used one that already existed). From here, I started to play with the typography. Because the project was related to music, I thought it could be visually interesting to mix and integrate the type with musical staff lines and convey the notion of something smooth that goes with the flow. I started to apply the effects, then made some print tests of different versions to see how it would look and work. Then I added the details and integrated the type on the graphic.

TOP:
NAUGHTY BOOK

BOTTOM:
BLOOD

BELOW:
MAJOR LEAGUE

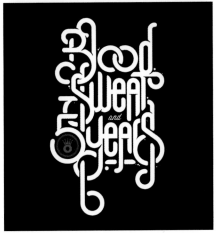

ALLISON CRUZADO
NEW YORK CITY
WWW.BEHANCE.NET/CRUZADO

ALLISON CRUZADO IS A GRAPHIC DESIGNER AND A COMPULSIVE LETTERER. IN 2007, SHE ATTENDED ALTOS DE CHAVÓN, LA ESCUELA DE DISEÑO, IN THE DOMINICAN REPUBLIC, WHERE SHE MAJORED IN COMMUNICATION DESIGN. UPON GRADUATING IN 2009, SHE RECEIVED A DEAN'S SCHOLARSHIP TO PARSONS, THE NEW SCHOOL FOR DESIGN. FOR THE PAST TWO YEARS, WHILE TRAVELING BETWEEN THE DOMINICAN REPUBLIC AND NEW YORK, SHE HAS WORKED FOR CLIENTS SUCH AS ORANGE, PIZZA HUT, GATORADE, AND NICKELODEON, AMONG MANY OTHERS. SHE LOVES TO CARRY A BLACK SKETCHBOOK EVERYWHERE AND SKETCH LETTERS IN HER SPARE TIME.

EL CATADOR LETTERING

When I work on lettering, I go directly to my sketchbook. The process is the same each time. I draw up a couple of rough sketches and choose the composition that works best. Then, I transfer it onto tracing paper, tweak the shapes and sizes, and perfect it as much as possible while it's still on paper. I try to work as cleanly as possible so that when I scan it onto the computer to digitize, there's not much clean up. Then I add texture and color to it.

LEFT:
EL CATADOR
LETTERING

LEFT:
LLEGÓ LA
NAVIDAD

RIGHT:
LLEGÓ LA
NAVIDAD

ABOVE:
STOLEN AWAY ON
THE 55TH & 3RD SKETCH

LEFT:
STOLEN AWAY ON
THE 55TH & 3RD

JOLUVIAN
MADRID
WWW.JOLUVIAN.COM

JOSE LUIS VIVAS ANDRADE, AKA JOLUVIAN, IS A GRAPHIC DESIGNER BASED IN MADRID. HE HAS TRAVELED TO MANY COUNTRIES, WORKING AND LEARNING ABOUT DIFFERENT CULTURES AND DIFFERENT ASPECTS OF DESIGN AND ILLUSTRATION. HE MAINLY FOCUSES ON CALLIGRAPHY AND ILLUSTRATION.

PLEASE TELL US ABOUT YOUR ART AND DESIGN BACKGROUND.

I'm not sure when I really decided to start doing this, but I remember two things: (1) My father and my grandfather had really beautiful handwriting; (2) When I was six or seven years old, I liked to paint, and there wasn't a day that I didn't draw something new. When I turned eight years old, my father decided to put me in a painting workshop that I stayed at for four years. After that, I did a few graffiti pieces and kept drawing illustrations either for myself or for friends. When I was older, I moved to Mérida, Spain, to start a graphic design career. Typography came later, when I was already living in Spain. A friend of mine suggested I start digging deeper into calligraphy, and I then got into typography. I think [my style development] has been a combination of family, time, growing up, and different environments.

LEFT:
SCRIPT HAND
LETTERING

OPPOSITE:
HERE'S TO THE
CRAZY ONES
SKETCH

Here's to the crazy ones

Joluvian

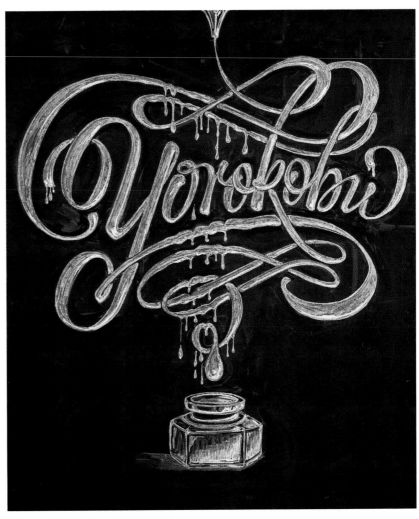

OPPOSITE/ABOVE:
YOROKOBU POSTERS

YOU HAVE CREATED BOTH A HAND-DRAWN PIECE AND A COMPUTER-BASED PIECE FOR THE YOROKOBU POSTER. WHAT'S YOUR REASONING BEHIND THIS?

After looking at the final work, I think my passion for perfection and for vectors invaded me and I wanted to do something else. Maybe it was inspiration, or maybe I just wanted to add another value—something people could have not only in a magazine but also on their living room walls. That is when I decided to create the second piece, the Yorokobu poster.

I started over in Illustrator, taking my time, making every detail. I worked around forty-five to fifty hours to finish it. I tested many things to convert my first magazine cover into a nice vector poster. After that, I could really say that I felt I had accomplished what I wanted. I had developed two techniques to show one message.

WHAT WOULD YOUR DREAM BRIEF FROM YOU DREAM BRAND BE AND WHY?

I really want to create a new logo for a sports team. I tried some years ago with a Venezuelan baseball team, but it didn't happen. I will be prepared to do it when the times comes because I grew up watching baseball and basketball with my father, and I have studied every sports team logo, uniform, and communication I have seen.

JAMES T. EDMONSON

SAN FRANCISCO

WWW.JAMESTEDMONDSON.COM

JAMES EDMONDSON IS A TYPE DESIGNER AND LETTERING ARTIST BASED IN SAN FRANCISCO. HAILING FROM THE GREAT CITY OF ARROYO GRANDE, CALIFORNIA, JAMES PRODUCES WORK INFLUENCED BY EVERYTHING FROM FRUIT CRATES TO AMATEUR GRAFFITI. IN HIS SPARE TIME, JAMES ENJOYS PLAYING MUSIC WITH HIS FRIENDS.

WOODS OF WISDOM LOGOTYPE

When working on the Woods of Wisdom lettering, I initially began sketching on isometric grid paper. This set the incline and overall geometric nature of the piece. After a monoline skeleton of the lettering was drawn, I brought the scan into Illustrator and traced over it with the pen tool to find the correct stroke width. After that, it was a matter of thinning out where the strokes flow into one another in order to keep an even tone throughout.

THIRD HALF DESIGN, CHAD MANN
MELBOURNE, AUSTRALIA
WWW.THIRDHALFDESIGN.COM

CHAD MANN IS A DESIGNER, ILLUSTRATOR, AND CREATIVE DIRECTOR OF THIRD HALF DESIGN IN MELBOURNE. ALTHOUGH MANN'S PROFESSIONAL EXPERIENCE INCLUDES DIRECTING CLOTHING LINES FOR THE WORLD'S LARGEST BRANDS AND SELF-PUBLISHED MAGAZINES, HIS CAREFULLY CRAFTED TYPOGRAPHIC WORK IS WHAT HE IS BEST KNOWN FOR. HIS TEXT AND DESIGN WORK HAS ELEMENTS OF BOTH SIMPLICITY AND CONGRUENCY, AND HIS FONTS ARE PULLED TOGETHER WITH REMARKABLE COHESION.

CONFETTI, CAKE & BUBBLES

Confetti, Cake & Bubbles was a collaboration between me and designer Shan Hoyne. The project began as thumbnail sketches and a digital rough of what I was hoping to achieve. From there we shared reference material, discussed the styling and treatments, and set in place a plan to get the best results.

All typography is refined in my sketchbook initially then vectorized in Illustrator. Shan then uses Cinema4D for the creation of 3-D models and the textured finishes. From there we worked together to refine the shapes, colors, textures, and shading until we were both happy with the end result.

LUKE LUCAS
MELBOURNE, AUSTRALIA
WWW.LUKELUCAS.COM

LUKE LUCAS IS AN ILLUSTRATOR, DESIGNER, AND TYPOGRAPHER WITH A SELF-MADE CAREER SPANNING TWO DECADES. IN THE LATE '90S, HE COCREATED *FOURINAROW*, AN INLINE SKATING MAGAZINE THAT WAS DISTRIBUTED WORLDWIDE. WITH TWO OTHER PARTNERS, HE STARTED *LIFELOUNGE*—SIMULTANEOUSLY A CREATIVE AGENCY, ONLINE CREATIVE CULTURE PORTAL, AND GLOSSY PRINT MAGAZINE. IT WAS THROUGH *LIFELOUNGE* THAT HE BEGAN TO EXPERIMENT WITH CONCEPTUAL ILLUSTRATIVE TYPOGRAPHY, CUSTOM LETTERING, AND TYPE DESIGN, AND IT WASN'T LONG BEFORE HE WAS ATTRACTING ILLUSTRATIVE TYPE BRIEFS FROM AGENCIES, PUBLISHERS, AND BRANDS ACROSS THE GLOBE. HIS REGULAR CLIENTS INCLUDE NIKE, TARGET USA, *ESQUIRE*, *THE NEW YORK TIMES*, AND *THE WASHINGTON POST*. IN 2011, AS A NEW FATHER, LUKE LEFT *LIFELOUNGE* TO SPEND MORE TIME WITH HIS FAMILY AND TO PURSUE A FULL-TIME FREELANCE CAREER FOCUSING ON TYPE.

BELOW:
HYPE TODAY

BELOW:
AMAZEBALLS

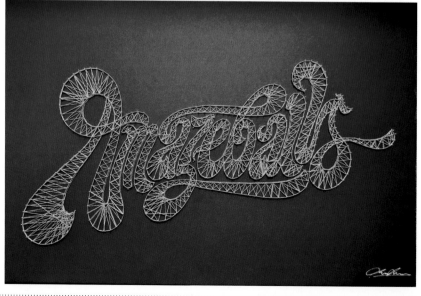

AMAZEBALLS

This piece was created for the 2012 group type show Who Shot the Serif at Sydney's He Made She Made Concept Gallery. The process for this piece, as with most of my work, was to commence with some initial sketches on paper to help visualize how the letters and ligature might interact. Once the lettering was decided, I made a scaled-up version of the type, placed it over several layers of black foam core that had been glued together to form a dense base, and began to insert dress pins along the edges of the letters. Once all the pins were inserted and my fingers stopped bleeding, I used French embroidery cotton to connect the pins by making overlapping lines in a repeated pattern across the face of the type. Once this stage was complete, I finished the work with a final outline in the same cotton to help define the letterforms.

BELOW:
THE NEW YORK TIMES SWEET & SAVORY

JORDAN METCALF
CAPE TOWN, SOUTH AFRICA
WWW.JORDAN-METCALF.COM

JORDAN METCALF IS A GRAPHIC DESIGNER, ILLUSTRATOR, AND ARTIST LIVING AND WORKING IN CAPE TOWN. AFTER WORKING FOR SEVERAL DESIGN STUDIOS DOING EVERYTHING FROM DESIGNING BOOKS TO DIRECTING FOR MOTION GRAPHICS, HE LEFT TO PURSUE AN INDEPENDENT DESIGN CAREER. HE HAS A STRONG FOCUS ON EXPERIMENTAL AND CRAFT-BASED CUSTOM LETTERING AND GRAPHIC DESIGN WORK AND HAS DONE WORK FOR CLIENTS SUCH AS ADOBE, *THE NEW YORK TIMES MAGAZINE*, AND NIKE, AND SHOWN WORK IN MANY LOCAL AND INTERNATIONAL EXHIBITIONS.

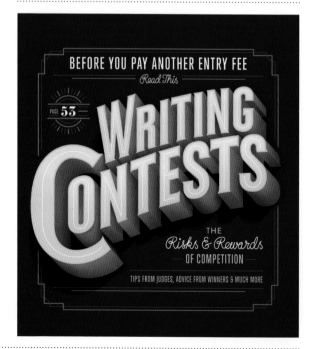

TOP:
YOU CAN'T TRUST MARKETERS

BOTTOM:
POETS & WRITERS MAGAZINE COVER

POPULAR MECHANICS
"BEST TIPS EVER" COVER

After an initial round of sketches, I refined a couple of directions to send to the client. We ended up combining elements that he liked from a couple of the sketches and roughly comped up the idea for the finished piece. I set to work creating the lettering in Illustrator. I like to work digitally and try to give myself as much freedom to tweak and improve and change things during the process. After getting a layout and execution style I was happy with, I sent images over to the client for approval. Once we had sign-off on the general design, I got into crafting all the small details that give the piece depth. I then took the final work into Photoshop to tweak colors and soften some of the crispness of the vectors using subtle textures and shading.

LEFT:
WHAT DO WE BELIEVE,
5280 MAGAZINE

CONTRIBUTORS

AARON VON FRETER
www.behance.net/vonfreter

ALEJANDRO GIRALDO
www.alejogiraldo.com

ALLISON CRUZADO
www.behance.net/cruzado

ANDRÉ BEATO
www.andrebeato.com

ANDY SMITH
www.asmithillustration.com

ASHLEY HOHNSTEIN
www.ashleyhohnstein.com

BEN JOHNSTON
www.behance.net/benjohnston

BEST DRESSED SIGNS
www.bestdressedsigns.com

C86, MATT LYON
www.c8six.com

CAROLYN SEWELL
www.carolynsewell.com

CHRIS PIASCIK
www.chrispiascik.com

CHRISTOPHER VINCA
www.behance.net/chrisvinca

COFFEE MADE ME DO IT,
SIMON ALANDER
www.coffeemademedoit.com

COMING SOON,
JIM VAN RAEMDONCK
www.coming-soon.be

CORY SAY
www.cargocollective.com/
corysay

DAN GRETTA
www.forefathersgroup.com

DANI LOUREIRO
www.behance.net/daniloureiro

DANIELLE IS HERE
www.danielleishere.com

DESIGN REFORM COUNCIL,
JACKKRIT ANANTAKUL
www.designreformcouncil.com

DINARA MIRTALIPOVA
www.mirdinara.com

EMMA DYSON
www.behance.net/
emmaleedyson

FRANCESCO POROLI
www.francescoporoli.it

GEORGIA HILL
www.georgiahill.tumblr.co

GINGER MONKEY, TOM LANE
www.gingermonkeydesign.com

GIULIA SANTOPADRE
www.giuliasantopadre.com

HOM SWEET HOM, LAUREN HOM
www.homsweethom.com

I LOVE DUST
www.ilovedust.com

JACKSON ALVES
www.jacksonalves.com

JAMES T. EDMONSON
www.jamestedmondson.com

JASON CARNE
www.jasoncarne.com

JEFF ROGERS
www.howdyjeff.com

JILL DE HAAN
www.jilldehaanart.prosite.com

JOEL FELIX
www.joelfelix.com

JOLUVIAN
www.joluvian.com

JON CONTINO
www.joncontino.com

JORDAN METCALF
www.jordan-metcalf.com

JORDI RINS
www.jordirins.com

JUANA LAXAGUE AND
VALERIA RUIZ-SCHULZE
www.behance.net/JuanaLaxague
www.behance.net/
ValeriaRuizSchulze

KENDRICK KIDD
www.kendrickkidd.com

LEANDRO SENNA
www.leandrosenna.com

LINZIE HUNTER
www.linziehunter.co.uk

LUKE LUCAS
www.lukelucas.com

MARTIN SCHMETZER
www.martinschmetzer.com

MARY KATE MCDEVITT
www.marykatemcdevitt.com

MATTHEW TAPIA
www.matthewtapia.com

MWM GRAPHICS,
MATT W. MOORE
www.mwmgraphics.com

NATE WILLIAMS
www.n8w.com

NEIL BEECH
www.behance.net/neilbeech

NO ENTRY DESIGN
www.noentrydesign.com

OPERA78, FIODOR SUMKIN
www.cargocollective.com/
opera78

OZAN KARAKOC
www.ozankarakoc.com

PANCO SASSANO
www.pancoart.com.ar

PAUL THURLBY
www.paulthurlby.com

RYAN FEERER
www.ryanfeerer.com

SAMUEL JACQUES
www.sjacques.com

SARAH A. KING
www.sarahaking.com

SEB LESTER
www.seblester.co.uk

SÉRGIO BERGOCCE
www.sergiobergocce.com

SIGN-FIDELITY,
CARL FREDRIK ANGELL
www.signfidelity.com

SIMON WALKER
www.simonwalkertype.com

STEPH SAYS HELLO,
STEPHANIE BAXTER
www.stephsayshello.co.uk

STEVE SIMPSON
www.stevesimpson.com

STUDIO AIRPORT
www.studio-airport.nl

THIRD HALF DESIGN,
CHAD MANN
www.thirdhalfdesign.com

TIMBA SMITS
www.timbasmits.com

TOBIAS HALL
www.tobias-hall.co.uk

TOMASZ BIERNAT
www.tomaszbiernat.us

VAULT49
www.vault49.com

VELCROSUIT, ADAM HILL
www.velcrosuit.com

WASTE STUDIO,
NORMAN HAYES
www.wastestudio.com

XESTA STUDIO, HUGO MOURA
www.xestastudio.com

Y&G
www.be.net/yaniguille

SECTION 2
DRAWING TYPE
INTRODUCTION

HERE IS WHERE I WANT TO ENCOURAGE YOU TO GET BACK TO BASICS. DRAWING TYPE CAN OPEN YOUR MIND TO A HUGE RANGE OF POSSIBILITIES, COMBINING BOTH HAND-DRAWN GRAPHICS AND DIGITAL TECHNIQUES. THERE ARE THIRTY TYPE SPECIMEN SHEETS DIVIDED INTO FOUR CATEGORIES TO HELP YOU GET STARTED: SERIF, SANS SERIF, SCRIPT, AND DISPLAY, EACH CONTAINING BOTH UPPERCASE AND LOWERCASE LETTERFORMS FROM A RANGE OF TYPEFACES. THE IDEA IS TO USE THESE SPECIMEN SHEETS AND TRACE THE LETTERS USING TRACING OR LAYOUT PAPER. AFTER YOU HAVE TRACED THE VARIOUS TYPEFACES A FEW TIMES, YOU WILL BEGIN TO KNOW THE DETAILS AND CHARACTERISTICS OF EACH TYPEFACE. ONCE YOU HAVE SPENT TIME DRAWING AND FEEL CONFIDENT TRACING TYPE, I ENCOURAGE YOU TO STOP TRACING AND JUST BEGIN TO DRAW LETTERFORMS WITHOUT THE AID OF THE SHEETS. OVER TIME, YOU CAN WATCH YOUR WORK AND STYLE DEVELOP AS YOU PRACTICE CREATING

TYPE CATEGORIES

HERE IS A BREAKDOWN AND BRIEF DESCRIPTION OF EACH CATEGORY.

SERIF

A serif is a semistructural detail on the ends of some of the strokes that make up letters and symbols. Serif typefaces are more legible than sans serifs at smaller point sizes. There are four font subtypes in the serif font family: old style, transitional, modern, and slab serif. Often, serif typefaces are used to give a feeling of nostalgia, trust, and heritage.

SANS SERIF

"Sans serif" comes from the French word *sans*, meaning "without." Sans serif typefaces tend to look more modern and can be great for grabbing attention. The characteristics between sans serif fonts can be quite subtle, but the more you draw them, the more you can appreciate those differences.

SCRIPT

Script typefaces mimic historical or modern handwriting styles that look as if written with different styles of writing instruments, from calligraphy pens to ballpoint pens. Typical characteristics of script typefaces are connected or nearly connected flowing letterforms, and slanted, rounded characters. Scripts can give a more welcoming feel, a more nostalgic look, or a more up-market, elegant feel, depending on what style font you chose.

DISPLAY

Display typefaces are probably the broadest category and include the most variation. The main characteristic is that they're unsuitable for body copy because of their exaggerated features and heavier weights, which become illegible at small sizes; therefore, display typefaces are best reserved for headlines or other short copy that needs to draw attention.

LETTERFORM ANATOMY

APERTURE

The aperture is the partially enclosed, somewhat rounded negative space (white space) in some characters such as *n*, *C*, *S*, the lower part of *e*, or the upper part of a two-story *a*.

APEX

The point at the top of a character, such as the uppercase *A*, where the left and right strokes meet is the apex. The apex may be a sharp point or be blunted or rounded, and is an identifying feature for some typefaces.

ARM

The arm of a letter is the horizontal stroke on some characters, such as *E* and *F*, that does not connect to a stroke or stem at one or both ends.

ASCENDER

The upward vertical stem on some lowercase letters, such as *h* and *b*, that extends above the x-height is the ascender. The height of the ascenders is an identifying characteristic of many typefaces.

TERMINAL

The terminal is a type of curve. Many sources consider a terminal to be just the straight or curved end (not including a serif) of any stroke.

BAR

The horizontal stroke across the middle of uppercase *A* and *H* is a bar. The horizontal or sloping stroke enclosing the bottom of the "eye" of an *e* is also a bar.

BILATERAL SERIFS

A bilateral serif is a serif that extends out from both sides of a main stroke.

BOWL

The curved part of the character that encloses the circular or curved parts of some letters such as *d*, *b*, *o*, *D*, and *B* is the bowl.

CROSS STROKE

The horizontal stroke across the stem of a lowercase *t* or *f* is a cross stroke. Although the terms are often used interchangeably, the cross stroke differs from an arm and a crossbar in that it intersects, or crosses over, the stem.

DESCENDER

The portion of some lowercase letters, such as *g* and *y*, that extends or descends below the baseline is the descender.

SHOULDER

The shoulder is the curved stroke aiming downward from a stem, such as the curve at the beginning of the leg in an *m*.

STEM

The stem is the main, usually vertical, stroke of a letterform.

STROKE

The main diagonal portion of a letterform, such as in *N*, *M*, or *y*, is the stroke. The stroke is secondary to the main stem.

SWASH

A swash is a typographical flourish on a glyph, kind of an exaggerated serif. Historically, capital swash characters, which extended to the left, were often used to begin sentences.

TOOLS

PENCIL

The pencil is a very important, but often overlooked, tool to use instead of the computer. It is good for many uses, from planning layouts and ideas all the way to completing final designs.

ERASERS

I try not to erase much in early stages of idea development and planning so I can let my ideas just flow, but once I've established an idea, I erase as a way to edit myself and get to the final design.

TRACING AND LAYOUT PAPER

I use these a lot, and I hope you will, too, when in the exercises section of this book. Tracing type is a great way to understand each detail of each letter within a typeface. I use layout paper to develop my designs and to try different options without hindering my original drawing.

INK AND PAINT

Changing up your media is a great way to experiment with different aesthetics. Doing so also leads to new ideas and avenues. So get messy!

BRUSHES AND MARKERS

Marks vary with every type of brush or marker used. This is all about trial and error. Brushes and brush pens are great for expressive, flowing marks. Markers can give a very strong, structured, and considered feel.

PRINTER AND SCANNER

These machines are essential for taking your designs to the screen, as well as for developing your ideas. A common practice is to scan an early design to screen, work it up, print it, work on it by hand again, and then scan for final touches.

VECTOR-BASED PROGRAM

Working with vectors is great for resizing work without losing quality. Working with vector graphics can give your work a much more digital and clinical feel compared to pixel-based graphics. Vectors can be great when working with typefaces and certain styles of illustration.

PIXEL-BASED PROGRAM

In a pixel-based program, you can add textures, photography, or digitally draw on top of your work. These programs allow for a lot of alterations, but be sure to get your dimensions right at the start.

FONTLAB OR SIMILAR FONT-EDITING PROGRAM

If you want to create your own working font from the letters you create, instead of hand-setting everything, you can use a font editing program such as FontLab, which will turn your letters into a fully working font.

METHOD

HERE IS A QUICK BREAKDOWN OF SOME BASIC STEPS TO HELP YOU GET STARTED WITH THE TYPE SHEETS. THE IDEA HERE IS, RATHER THAN TRYING TO DRAW THE TYPEFACES, YOU TRACE THEM; JUST FOLLOW THE LINES, LOOK AT THE SERIFS, AND NOTICE THE THICKNESS OF THE LETTERS. THIS WILL HELP YOU UNDERSTAND THE BASICS OF EACH LETTERFORM WITHIN EACH TYPEFACE AND GIVE YOU A GREATER APPRECIATION FOR WHAT MAKES CERTAIN TYPEFACES UNIQUE.

STEP 1:

TEAR OUT A SPECIMEN SHEET

STEP 2:

GRAB YOUR LAYOUT OR TRACING PAPER

STEP 3:

TRACE YOUR TYPEFACES

STEP 4:

SCAN YOUR TRACED TYPEFACE

Once you have scanned your typeface, separate the letters and start setting words letter by letter; this will help you appreciate kerning (the space between letters) and leading (the space between lines of type). Trying different layouts within one design will help you understand how to gain balance in your design. Don't be afraid to add illustrations or details—you can always take them out later.

From this point on, the possibilities are endless. There are multiple styles and treatments you can apply to your design. Then, once you are confident enough, forget tracing and begin to draw your words and designs freehand—only then will it become an original piece of work. I urge you use this method for personal use only: Anything you create in this way isn't original, and you would be infringing on another artist's copyright. I classify this method as a personal experimentation so that you can better understand typography and start learning and developing your own style that then can be used to create original work further down the line.

PLAYFUL TYPE
EXERCISES
YOU SHOULD ATTEMPT THESE EXERCISES ONCE YOU HAVE DRAWN YOUR OWN ALPHABETS AND HAVE A NICE, READY-TO-USE COLLECTION.

EXERCISE: CREATE A FUN, ILLUSTRATIVE PIECE USING SOME VARIED AND SLIGHTLY LESS CONSTRAINED TECHNIQUES. COMBINING SOME ILLUSTRATION AND BRIGHT COLORS ARE KEY TO CREATING A PLAYFUL FEEL.

Choose a phrase, quote, or collection of words you like, and then using the specimen sheets provided, scan in your letters and begin to set the words by hand. Don't feel that you need to use every step listed—just choose ones that suit your idea.

Experiment with your line quality. Rather than just straight lines, try wavy, spiky, or dotted lines—all of this will help add to the playful nature.

Use a whole range of typefaces—don't just stick to one. Get creative with the typefaces you choose.

Add patterns and geometric shapes within your type for added detail.

Use small illustrations that relate to your content and try to make them interact with words or part of your design.

Try fitting type to a certain shape or illustration to help aid your message.

Experiment with different media, from pencils and markers to brush and ink. Each medium has its own characteristics, so find what works best for you.

The WORST MISTAKE MISTAKE IS TO MAKE NOT ANY

VINTAGE TYPE
EXERCISES

EXERCISE: CREATE A VINTAGE FEEL WITH TYPE YOU'VE CREATED FROM THE SPECIMEN SHEETS PROVIDED. FOLLOW THESE STEPS TO HELP YOU GET AN AUTHENTIC VINTAGE STYLE.

Set your words using a typeface of your choice. Often, scripts or serifs are the most authentic faces to use, but they are not mandatory here.

Use Photoshop or Illustrator to help you set the words and then create a layout. Look at arching your words or shearing them vertically to keep them from being on a straight line.

Placing words in banners or block shapes adds to the vintage look. Print your word and try drawing a banner around it.

Borders and flourishes are great details you can explore. Try adding them to your design, but use them sparingly.

Try to include more little details within your piece, such as dates, place names, or sources. This is great secondary information to help inform the viewer of the hierarchy involved.

IF YOU DON'T BUILD *Your Dream* SOMEONE ELSE WILL HIRE YOU TO BUILD THEIRS

CONTEMPORARY TYPE
EXERCISES

CONTEMPORARY TYPE IS A VERY BROAD SUBJECT, SO FOR THIS EXERCISE I LOOK AT IT AS TYPE CREATED DIGITALLY, USING EITHER VECTORS OR PIXELS, DEPENDING ON THE DESIRED OUTCOME. I WOULD LOOK AT COMPLETING THIS EXERCISE ONCE YOU HAVE SPENT TIME DRAWING TYPE FROM THE SPECIMEN SHEETS AND CREATING TYPOGRAPHIC LAYOUTS OF YOUR OWN.

EXERCISE: DRAW A LAYOUT BY HAND AND THEN TRACE YOUR DESIGN IN ILLUSTRATOR AND EXPERIMENT WITH DIFFERENT TECHNIQUES.

Trace the piece in Illustrator until you have re-created everything you drew on paper.

Try layering parts and adding details, such as shadows below the type, to give more depth and a realistic lighting feel.

Play with customizing part of your traced letters to see what else can be made. You have a digital version now, so go wild.

Add inner highlights and shadows within your script typefaces to give a rounded feel.

Try vector shading in various elements of your piece to add a 3-D feel.

Take your vector design and play with the color combinations, then take it in to Photoshop. Here, you can add textures and photographic elements and go to town on the finishing.

Try mocking up any of your designs onto posters, apparel, or merchandise. It's a great way to see your work come to life.

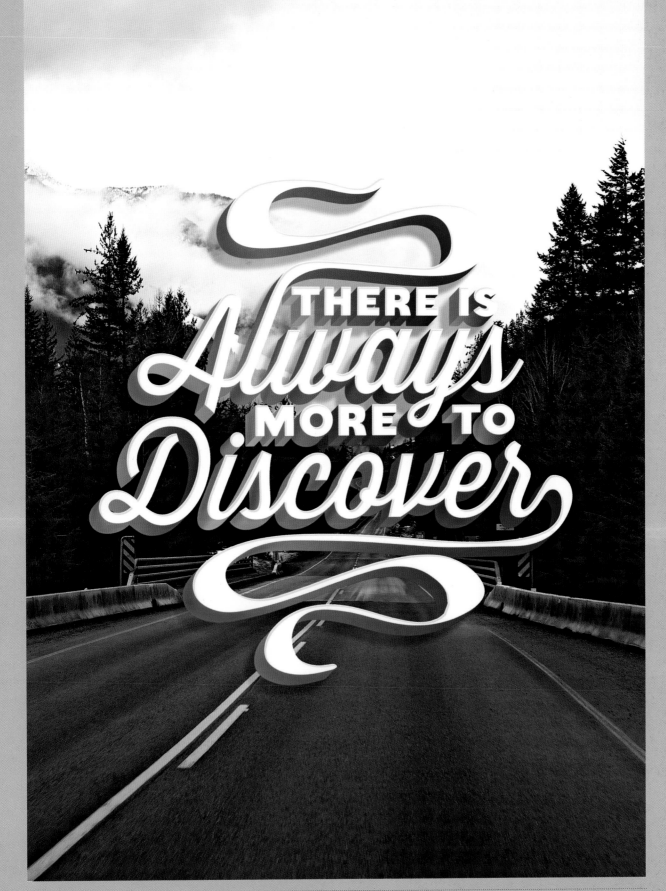

HAND-RENDERED TYPE
EXERCISES

EXERCISE: DRAW A TOTALLY HAND-RENDERED PIECE OF WORK. HERE, I AM TRYING TO ENCOURAGE YOU TO CREATE WORK WITHOUT THE USE OF THE SHEETS SO THIS CAN TRULY BE YOUR OWN ORIGINAL PIECE OF HAND-DRAWN TYPE.

Turn your page into a modular grid, or use gridded paper. This will help you keep letters in line and distribution easier to manage.

Write your words down in your own handwriting and create multiple layouts and compositions.

Once you have your basic layout sketched, scan it, and print it out multiple times as practice sheets. Here, you can vary your design direction without committing to one.

Try adding perspective to some of your words to make them really stand off the page, or you can add textures or patterns within certain letters.

Watch your x-heights, descenders, and ascenders when drawing. Use the grid to help keep them all at the same size.

Use a range of pencils to shade some parts of your work to add more depth.

Extend script faces by adding swash elements to descenders or ascenders, or elongate other parts of a word for a more custom feel.

SPECIMEN SHEETS

CATEGORY: SANS SERIF
Typeface: ITC Avante Garde Gothic
Weight: Demi
Pt size: 91

CATEGORY: SANS SERIF
Typeface: ITC Kabel
Weight: Medium
Pt size: 87

CATEGORY: SANS SERIF
Typeface: FF Din
Weight: Medium
Pt size: 88

CATEGORY: SANS SERIF
Typeface: Helvetica
Weight: Medium
Pt size: 84

CATEGORY: SERIF
Typeface: Adobe Caslon Pro
Weight: Bold
Pt size: 69

CATEGORY: SERIF
Typeface: Times
Weight: Regular
Pt size: 90

CATEGORY: SERIF
Typeface: ITC Lubalin Graph
Weight: Demi
Pt size: 83

CATEGORY: SERIF
Typeface: Bodoni
Weight: Roman
Pt size: 84

CATEGORY: SCRIPT
Typeface: Thirsty Script
Weight: Regular
Pt size: 75

CATEGORY: SCRIPT
Typeface: Lavanderia
Weight: Sturdy
Pt size: 70

CATEGORY: SCRIPT
Typeface: Aphrodite Slim
Weight: Text
Pt size: 53

CATEGORY: SCRIPT
Typeface: Grand Hotel
Weight: Regular
Pt size: 91

CATEGORY: DISPLAY
Typeface: Sobek
Weight: Regular
Pt size: 95

CATEGORY: DISPLAY
Typeface: Geared Slab
Weight: Regular
Pt size: 90

CATEGORY: DISPLAY
Typeface: Gordon
Weight: Black
Pt size: 128

CATEGORY: DISPLAY
Typeface: Brothers
Weight: Regular
Pt size: 90

CATEGORY:
SANS SERIF

Typeface:
ITC Avant Garde
Gothic

Weight:
Demi

Size:
91 pt

abcdefgh
ijklmnopq
rstuvwxyz
ABCDEFGH
IJKLMNOPQ
RSTUVWXYZ
1234567890
!@£$%&*()+

abcdefgh
ijklmnopq
rstuvwxyz
ABCDEFGH
IJKLMNOPQ
RSTUVWXYZ
1234567890
!@£$%&*()+

CATEGORY:
SANS SERIF

Typeface:
FF Din

Weight:
Medium

Size:
88 pt

abcdefghij
klmnopqrs
tuvwxyz
ABCDEFGHI
JKLMNOPQR
RSTUVWXYZ
1234567890
!@£$%&*()+

SPECIMEN SHEETS

CATEGORY:
SANS SERIF

Typeface:
Helvetica

Weight:
Medium

Size:
84 pt

abcdefghijk
lmnopqrstu
vwxyzABCD
EFGHIJKLM
NOPQRSTU
VWXYZ1234
567890!@£$
%&*()_+

SPECIMEN SHEETS

CATEGORY:
SERIF

Typeface:
Adobe Caslon Pro

Weight:
Bold

Size:
69 pt

abcdefghijkl
mnopqrstuv
wxyzABCDE
FGHIJKLMN
OPQRSTUV
WXYZ1234
567890!@£$
%&*()_+

SPECIMEN SHEETS

CATEGORY:
SERIF

Typeface:
TImes

Weight:
Regular

Size:
90 pt

abcdefghijkl
mnopqrstuv
wxyzABCDE
FGHIJKLM
NOPQRSTU
VWXYZ123
4567890!@£
$%&*()+

CATEGORY:	Typeface:	Weight:	Size:
SERIF	ITC Lubalin Graph	Demi	83 pt

abcdefghij
klmnopqrst
uvwxyzABC
DEFGHIJKL
MNOPQRS
TUVWXYZ
1234567890
!@£$%&*()+

SPECIMEN SHEETS

CATEGORY:
SERIF

Typeface:
Bodoni

Weight:
Roman

Size:
84 pt

abcdefghijk
lmnopqrstu
vwxyzABCD
EFGHIJKL
MNOPQRS
TUVWXYZ
1234567890
!@£$%&*()+

CATEGORY:	Typeface:	Weight:	Size:
SCRIPT	Thirsty Script	Regular	75 pt

abcdefghijkl
mnopqrstuvw
xyzABCDEF
GHIJKLM
NOPQRSTUV
WXYZ123456
7890@£$%&*+

CATEGORY:
SCRIPT

Typeface:
Lavanderia

Weight:
Sturdy

Size:
70 pt

SPECIMEN SHEETS

CATEGORY:
SCRIPT

Typeface:
Aphrodite Slim

Weight:
Text

Size:
53 pt

SPECIMEN SHEETS

CATEGORY:
SCRIPT

Typeface:
Grand Hotel

Weight:
Regular

Size:
91 pt

abcdefghijklm
nopqrstuvwxyz
ABCDEFGHIJ
KLMNOPQRST
UVWXYZ 12345
67890@£$%&*+

CATEGORY:
DISPLAY

Typeface:
Sobek

Weight:
Regular

Size:
95 pt

ABCDEFGHIJKL
MNOPQRST
UVWXYZ123
4567890
!@£$%&*()+

| CATEGORY: | Typeface: | Weight: | Size: |
| DISPLAY | Geared Slab | Regular | 90 pt |

abcdefghijklm
nopqrstuvwxyz
ABCDEFGHIJKL
MNOPQRSTUVW
XYZ 1234567890
!@£$%&*[]_+

CATEGORY:	Typeface:	Weight:	Size:
DISPLAY	Gordon	Black	128 pt

ABCDEFG
HIJKLMN
OPQRSTU
VWXYZ12
34567890
!@£$%&*
()_+

abcdefghijkl
mnopqrstuv
wxyzABCDEF
GHIJKLMNO
PQRSTUVWX
YZ 12345678
90!@£$%&*